Learning To Live In
God's Sweet Spot

*From the Frustration of
Running on Empty to the
Fulfillment of Life Overflowing*

Learning To Live In
God's Sweet Spot
*From the Frustration of
Running on Empty to the
Fulfillment of Life Overflowing*

Daron Garmon

XULON PRESS

Xulon Press
2301 Lucien Way #415
Maitland, FL 32751
407.339.4217
www.xulonpress.com

© 2019 by Daron Garmon

All rights reserved solely by the author. The author guarantees all contents are original and do not infringe upon the legal rights of any other person or work. No part of this book may be reproduced in any form without the permission of the author. The views expressed in this book are not necessarily those of the publisher.

Unless otherwise indicated, Scripture quotations taken from the Holy Bible, New Living Translation (NLT). Copyright ©1996, 2004, 2007 by Tyndale House Foundation. Used by permission of Tyndale House Publishers, Inc.

Scripture quotations taken from the Amplified Bible (AMP). Copyright © 1954, 1958, 1962, 1964, 1965, 1987 by The Lockman Foundation. Used by permission. All rights reserved.

Scripture quotations taken from the Contemporary English Version (CEV). Copyright © 1995 American Bible Society. Used by permission. All rights reserved.

Scripture quotations taken from the English Standard Version (ESV). Copyright © 2001 by Crossway, a publishing ministry of Good News Publishers. Used by permission. All rights reserved.

Scripture quotations taken from The Message (MSG). Copyright © 1993, 1994, 1995, 1996, 2000, 2001, 2002. Used by permission of NavPress Publishing Group. Used by permission. All rights reserved.

Scripture quotations taken from the King James Version (KJV) – public domain.

Scripture quotations taken from the Holy Bible, New International Version (NIV). Copyright © 1973, 1978, 1984, 2011 by Biblica, Inc.™. Used by permission. All rights reserved.

Printed in the United States of America.

ISBN-13: 978-1-54566-086-7

TABLE OF CONTENTS

Special Thanks vii

Chapter 1:   It Worked for Me. 9
Chapter 2:   Selah-Vie 22
Chapter 3:   The Pattern Puzzle: How the Story Usually Unfolds. . . .30
Chapter 4:   What's the Point of a History Lesson?. 44
Chapter 5:   In _____ We Trust. 54
Chapter 6:   Good to Go. 63
Chapter 7:   If God Really Cared About Me 77
Chapter 8:   Here I Go Again On My Own. 87
Chapter 9:   Bull in a China Shop. 97
Chapter 10: Can Life Get Any Worse?. 103
Chapter 11: I Give Up!. 110
Chapter 12: Here I AM to Save the Day 118
Chapter 13: Home Sweet Home 126
Chapter 14: Drastic Measures, Baby Steps. 133
Chapter 15: Pray, Pray, Pray (and then pray some more) 143
Chapter 16: Who's Your Daddy?. 176

Chapter 17: Attitude of Gratitude................................ 187

Chapter 18: Hope for Your Future............................... 196

Chapter 19: Forgive(n)ess 222

Chapter 20: Finding Your Way.................................. 246

Chapter 21: Living Life on Purpose 258

Endnotes.. 271

SPECIAL THANKS

My greatest thanks is to God. He inspired every concept in this book. Though it took me a decade to begin writing, God was persistent in His calling on my life. Once I decided to Surrender to God's best for my life and chose to begin living in His *Sweet Spot*, He downloaded the framework of this book into my head with a matter of hours. Once I started writing, however, it took me a bit over a year for me to put His thoughts into words, as I needed to process and live out the thoughts He was giving me. I am humbled by the thought that God would use me to deliver such a timely, transitional, and powerful message. I will always be grateful to God for giving me His direction.

I also want to thank my mother, Carol Garmon, for her input on the book, her inspiration, and her diligence in encouraging me to be the influencer in people's lives that God's desires me to be.

Additionally, a dear friend, Michelle Bowerman, has been a great influence on how this book flows. In writing this book, God used her in ways that I could not have accomplished on my own.

Thank you!

Chapter One

IT WORKED FOR ME…

"Do not think that what is hard for you to master is humanly impossible; but if a thing is humanly possible, consider it to be within your reach."
~ Marcus Aurelius, Meditations, VI, 19[1]

If you've ever felt run down, like you were running on fumes, or, even worse yet, like you were *run-out-of-gas, completely bone-dry, dead-on empty*, then I was probably the one who siphoned your tank and sucked every life-giving breath right out of your soul. I am truly sorry for putting you through that. I'm sorry for hurting you, numbing you, scarring you, and for leaving you confused, jaded, or worse.

When I was doing those things, I knew—deep within my soul—that I was barren on the inside. What I didn't recognize was that my empty cravings and disparity always led me to selfishly drain each and every person I'd ever cared about of everything they'd ever cared about.

Looking back, it's as if I was living my entire life inside the cylinder of a washing machine that was stuck on the spin cycle. I felt like your clothes look when the machine stops. I was pressed up against the wall, stuck, had an emptiness in the bottom of my well.

There was an occasional visitor to my realm of pity, but they never stayed for very long. *Why* no one stayed seems pretty self-explanatory, but let's suffice it to say that I had taken up residency in a place that no one ever wants to fall asleep dreaming about, let alone wake up to as a daily reality.

I didn't want to keep awakening in that same place any more than you do (take a moment and consider *your* own emptiness or pit). But, I didn't know how to get out.

I wanted out, but I felt so incredibly stuck in a quagmire of my own doings. I figured I'd just end up spending the rest of my life in my own (un)comfortable, reoccurring rut.

There were times, however, when I thought there was hope for my futile existence. A ray of sunshine would reach the bleakness of my heart. I'd catch glimpses of a better life. But, herein lies the problem: I was an ingenious master of taking generous portions of sunshine and turning them into a damaging hailstorm.

Have you ever exited a movie theater in the middle of the day, lost track of time, and forgotten the sun was still shining outside? You walk through the exit doors and suddenly your dilated eyes are invaded by the glare of sunshine. That's the way I felt when the radiant blessing of a sunshiny moment came my way. Instead of adjusting to the moment and trying to enjoy it, I'd squint my eyes, turn my head downward, and run away. Instead of soaking in that life-giving light, I'd run straight for the grim shelter of my ever-deepening hole.

There Has To Be A Better Place

After a while of feeling unworthy of anything good, my old patterns of destructiveness would raise their ugly heads. Some patterns I was aware

It Worked For Me...

of, but there were also grossly repetitive attitudes and actions that completely eluded my conscious brain.

Still, whether I was aware of the pattern or not, the predator in me would inevitably emerge. And, like a black widow spider, I would entangle yet another victim in my web of self-deception, sucking the life out of anyone and everyone I could snare.

I didn't want to keep landing there. I didn't want to keep doing things the way I'd always done, hurting one person after the other—while slowly self-destructing at the same time. I didn't want to go *there* again. In fact, I wanted to land in a completely different place (and stay there) so badly that I could taste the smell of it.

I had heard of this place, even wandered through it from time to time. The place where I wanted to be was what one English translation of the Bible calls the "secret place" of God.

> "He that *dwelleth* in the *secret place* of the most High shall *abide* under the shadow of the Almighty" (Psalm 91:1, KJV; *emphases mine*).

I coined my own phrase for the prospering and protective *secret place* of God many years ago. I discovered (and rediscovered) it when—occasionally—I'd stumble down the path less traveled, worn out and panting for a drop of what I knew God had to offer.

I call that secret place *"God's Sweet Spot."*

I wasn't usually there for very long. I did more *passing through* than visiting, let alone abiding or dwelling in this place of security and comfort. Each and every time, instead of making my home in God's refuge,

I'd end up doing the same things I'd always done—not only to people, but also to God.

Repeatedly, after a stint of bliss—living in God's sweetest of places—I'd settle into my old ways of bringing death to where there once was life. And, instead of taking any personal responsibility, I'd blame God, wives, girlfriends, family, friends, and foes alike. I always insisted that everyone had given up on me instead of sticking with me until I became the man I was destined to be.

I was only partially right. There really was a new me coming. Where I was gravely wrong was in believing that these cherished people had given up on me. The stark truth is that I had given up on myself. And, in order to feel anything that even closely resembled happiness or life, I begged and pleaded for "more, more, more" so much that, eventually, these people had nothing left to give. They hadn't given up; they were utterly depleted. They were *run-out-of-gas, completely bone-dry, dead-on empty*.

Each time I took someone's breath, instead of it filling my soul and bringing me life, I found myself as empty as those I was draining. In those moments, I'd cry out in utter anguish "Why me?" accusations toward God and expletive condemnation toward those who could no longer sustain me.

Momentary Reprieve

There were brief moments in time, however, when I knew I'd wallowed for far too long. These were the moments when I came face-to-face with my own shortcomings and all I wanted to do was drive a stake straight through the heart of the bloodsucking vampire I had become. I knew the crushing weight of the blame rested on *my* shoulders. It was during those moments when I wanted nothing more than to be set free from the living hell I woke up to and faced every morning.

During those sporadic times of deepest reflection, I'd often turn to Psalm 51 and pray every word of the first thirteen verses from my deepest, worn down place. When I got to verses 10-13, I would take a deep breath and hope—somehow hope—God would hear me this time.

> "Create in me a clean heart, O God. Renew a loyal spirit within me. Do not banish me from your presence, and don't take your Holy Spirit from me. *Restore to me the joy of your salvation*, and *make me willing* to obey you. Then I will teach your ways to rebels, and they will return to you" (Psalm 51:10-13, NLT; *emphases* mine).

I knew I couldn't save myself. And way too many people in my life had died a martyr's death trying to rescue me. I knew my only source of hope was for God to *restore to me the joy of* [His] *salvation*. And I'd tell myself that *if* He ever did rescue me and change me, I would fulfill the promise of teaching His ways to others who felt like there was no hope for lasting change, let alone fulfillment in life. I would open the doors—as God opened their hearts and eyes—to the kind of transformation He'd brought me through and then guide them directly into the restful, secret, and sweetest place of God's grace and goodness.

I had times of doubt as I wallowed in my own self-pity, but I knew when the answer to my prayers was made clear, God's revelation would bring with it hope, help, freedom, healing, and joy. So, I promised God if He ever brought me to that place—and showed me how I could learn to stay there, instead of returning to my old ruts of independence and rebellion—I'd share the hope I'd found with anyone and everyone who slightly resembled my reflection in their own mirrors. I promised to walk with them all the way into the loving arms of God. I'd do all of this *if* God would ever just listen to my cry. *"God, help me,"* was the continuous outpouring of my heart.

Unfortunately, instead of waiting for God to reveal Himself to me and open the door to my freedom, I began drifting further and further away from Him. As I did, I also became increasingly self-reliant. But my independent nature was just a premature indication of the monster I was yet to become.

You Can Fool Some Of The People, Some Of The Time

I tried to hide the weakest areas of my life from everyone. In fact, I became a master of disguise and fooled most of the people, most of the time. I even thought I could fool my wife, but I was only fooling myself.

At the time, I didn't recognize myself as a bloodsucking louse. From the outside, looking in, no one would have seen me as a villain. No one would have thought I was robbing my wife of every life-giving breath she tried to take. Even looking at her from my own, insider vantage-point, I had no idea *she knew* her breath was being taken from her until the very day she yanked my siphon away and declared she could no longer be married to me.

Just like that, everything—and I mean *everything*—came crashing down.

I was taken aback, to say the least. Sure, there had been fights. Some of them were quite frightful. But I chalked all of that up to bouts of drinking, not to my parasitic ways. Only in retrospect have I been able to see the error of the repeating patterns in my life.

Your personal, predictable patterns may differ from mine, but the inward confusion is often starkly similar. Can you pinpoint your pattern or patterns?

For me, I knew I was sucking on a bottle. That was evident. But had no idea I was also a life-sucking leech.

❖ **Mine May Be Different, But Yours Is The Same**

I guess you picked up on my *bottle-sucking*? I never mentioned my struggle with alcohol until now. And why now?

Addiction is an ugly monster that none of us would ever join ourselves to, at least not willingly. But it's something I struggled with for 30+ years before I finally saw the hand of God extended toward me—as it had been all along—and discovered the solution to all of my empty wandering.

Now, at this stage of my faith-journey, I don't blame *anything* on alcohol. First, because I am happy to say that alcohol no longer has control over me. And second—though equally important—I have come to realize addiction for what it is: a symptom of emptiness. Can addiction cause emptiness? Absolutely! More often, however, it is our emptiness that leads us to addictive behaviors.

What defines your emptiness? Not everyone who picks this book up and reads it struggles with an addiction. But we all have our struggles. What causes your inner turmoil? You may already know the source of your emptiness. I definitely knew mine. And, for a greater portion of my life than I wish to admit, I was the emptiest of all living souls.

These days, however, I have a keen awareness of God's patience and unfailing love. I've learned not only to visit with God, but have also found the secret to resting in His full-time presence. It's that awareness that presents itself in my every day, fruitful, and overflowing kind of life. A life I'd only dreamt of before.

No. Not all days or breaths are that fantastical. But you'll be surprised—as you journey with me—how many breaths and days are.

Between Then and Now

Before I got to where I am now, however, I managed to destroy three marriages and damage many other vital relationships along the way, including my relationship with my daughter. You'd think that after several disastrous relational crashes I would have made some significant changes; but, at the time, I had no clue. I had no clue that the kind of freedom you'll discover in the chapters to come was within my grasp.

It was when I came to the realization I was losing (if not, already lost) my daughter that I decided I wanted to do more than just drive by or pass through the *secret place* of God. I wanted to *dwell* there. I knew my only hope was in the deliverance and refuge of that place I'd known before, but had always walked away from: *God's Sweet Spot*.

❖ **Hopeful Expectation**

Several years prior, when I was on an extended stay with God and was investing in my relationship with Him, I adopted this passage of Scripture as my life's mantra:

> "I **waited patiently** for the Lord to help me, and he turned to me and heard my cry. **He lifted me** out of the pit of despair, out of the mud and the mire. **He set my feet on solid ground** and **steadied me** as I walked along. He has given me **a new song to sing**, a hymn of praise

to our God. **Many will see what he has done** and be amazed. **They will put their trust in the Lord**" (Psalm 40:1-3, NLT; *emphases mine*).

Though I lost track of those verses while I was out breathing other people's air for several more years, the potential loss of my daughter lead me to the hardest, yet easiest, decision I had ever made. I decided to check myself in to an addiction rehabilitation facility and get some help.

It was at this facility I began reading a book that my mom had given me—but that I had never taken the time to read in the past. The book was Beth Moore's *"Get Out of that Pit*[2]*"* and is based on the premise of my since forgotten mantra. The author's conviction is that God is the only one who can pull us out of our pit, that Jesus is our firm foundation outside of that pit, and that our deepest and heartfelt cries *are* heard—and answered—by the lover of our souls.

I began crying out, in *hopeful expectation*, which is really a better translation than "waited patiently" in the above verse. The original Hebrew text of Psalm 40:1 suggests an expectant and active period of waiting.

You see, *hopeful expectation* differs from simply hoping God will hear you this time. It's anticipating the good things God has in store for you and fully trusting that His artistic rendition of your future is better than anything you could ever ask for or imagine. *Hopeful expectation is acting on what you already know to be good and true, while you wait for God's best to take shape.*

I practiced everything I was learning. I cried with confessions; I called out for hope, direction, and the grace to sustain me. I knew I had been set free from the power of sin and death, but I wanted that knowledge to reach my heart and forever transform my life (see Romans 8:1-8, Amplified Version).

I wanted to become the kind of person who pumps fuel into others rather than siphoning it. I longed for the opportunity to teach God's ways to rebels in order that they might return to Him (see aforementioned Psalm 51:13). And, I awaited the recognition of change, from the perspective of others, so that they might be in awe and put their trust in the Lord (see aforementioned Psalm 40:3).

❖ Would You Bet On Me?

When important heart changes began to take place in my life, not everybody noticed. I saw the change. I knew I was growing. But everything about me wasn't instantaneously transformed. There were times when I jumped right back into the cylinder of that spinning washing machine and acted within my deeply engrained patterns.

During those spinning moments, it's easy for people to become skeptical of any enduring change. Please don't be discouraged. The change within you will eventually overflow into the lives of others in relevant and distinguishable ways. If you feel yourself becoming discouraged as you take this journey into fulfillment, keep in mind the words of the Apostle Paul when he said,

> "Not that I have already attained, or am already perfected; but I press on, that I may lay hold of that for which Christ Jesus has also laid hold of me" (Philippians 3:12, NKJV).

I knew God had a purpose for me, and I was opening my heart to Him more and more each day. At last, I was feeling alive again. More alive than I'd ever felt. Still, I knew I hadn't reached the nirvana of walking in God's absolute best. I needed to press on.

Having my feet *"on solid ground"* was a gratifying place to rest—for a while—but I wanted to learn how to walk on the solid foundation of Jesus Christ each and every day. I determined to tightly grasp God's hand, allowing Him to teach me what it meant to be "steadied" as I traversed life's journey (see aforementioned Psalm 40:2).

I knew I wasn't demonstrating the kind of life that would strike awe in people's hearts—yet. But, I knew that day was coming. I knew that when I was ready, God would open the doors for me to reflect His transformative powers to people who knew they desperately needed a similar change to take place in their own lives (see aforementioned Psalm 40:3).

Still, I knew there was a missing piece. I knew God was opening the doors of my future, one step at a time. I also knew that before I could get to the part where people were in awe of the changes in me and chose to follow a similar design for change in their own lives, I was missing the vital step of a *new song to sing* (see aforementioned Psalm 40:3). I tried to adopt several theme songs over time, but my release into the world of pointing others to my source of change always seemed to be prolonged.

Cue Entrance, Stage Right

The missing piece was finally put in place when I first heard the *new song* for my lips—*a hymn of praise to our God*. Instantaneously, I was propelled through that particular stage of my awakening and given the confidence to write this book. The song of freedom and release I heard was Crowder's *"All My Hope."* My heart resonated with the lyrics of that song, from start to finish, but the verse I couldn't wait to sing along with—at the top of my lungs and from the depth of my soul—made my current and *steadfast* path crystal clear:

"I'm no stranger to prison.
I've worn shackles and chains.
But I've been freed and forgiven.
And I'm not going back; I'll never be the same[3]."

That, my hopeful friend, is why I wrote this book. I want to walk with you into the freedom God has had planned for you since before you were ever born. I want to illustrate to you what I've learned along my journey, and show you the same Biblical principles that continue to fill my life with trust, joy, and contentment. I want you to learn, for yourself, that *you never have to go back* to whatever has been holding you down. As you practice the precepts we'll be discussing as we take this journey with God, *you'll never be the same.*

In fact, I am confident you will begin to see changes right away. Almost immediately, you'll feel like the mountain of baggage you've been carrying, pushing, pulling and even dragging around with you is dissipating with each day you take another step toward the hope and healing that is being offered.

Even though your story may seem—on the outside—entirely different from mine, hope and fulfillment are in store for you too. You may not have an addictive nature at all. You may have never noticed a trail of fallen martyrs, left in the dust of your destructive patterns. Perhaps, instead, your struggle is with fear, past failures, dead-end relationships, anger, mistrust, lust, depression, anxiety, or all of the above. Whatever your repetitive cycle of emotions and subsequent actions—I know, because I have been there too—the most common end result is an overwhelming and exhausted sense of frustration. Frustration with yourself. Frustration with others. Frustration because you keep finding yourself in the same place, predicament, or circumstance over and over again.

Well, the frustration ends here! The greatest thing about my journey toward healing, joy, and contentment is that if God can pick me up out of the utter emptiness and decay I found myself deeply mired within, He is surely able to transform whatever pattern you may be stuck in and propel your life *"from the frustration of running-on-empty to the fulfillment of life overflowing."*

So, let's take a walk together—just you, me, and the lover of our souls—and learn how to live in *"God's Sweet Spot."* *Everything* better awaits us!

Chapter Two

SELAH-VIE

"What are YOU going to do about it?"
~ Me, to my dad, at the age of seventeen

Do you remember the colorfully illustrated picture on the last page of the whimsical tales read to you as a child? The picture I remember is one of a couple riding off into the sunset in a horse-drawn carriage.

Can you see it? Do you ever dream of it? Do you ever "wish upon a star" in hopes the fairytale will become true in your own life?

How did the last line of those stories always end? Go ahead, say it out loud: *"And they lived Happily Ever After."*

For many of us, the sunset we're riding into isn't as glorious. Instead, we seem to be on the fast-track to divorce, alienation, frustration, unemployment, foreclosure, addiction, emotional bruising, brokenness, implosion, and even death. At best, we try to elude the seemingly inevitable by finding yet another way to temporarily escape our problems.

But, *what if* the radiant hues of that "happily ever after" sunset really do exist? What if—somehow, some way—that hopeful journey became our confident reality? Then the stories we would tell today's children would not be tall-tales of fantastical lands. Instead, the legacy we'd share would empower the youngest toddler, the most rebellious teen, ourselves, and everyone between and beyond to embrace *the promise* of a brighter future.

Sadly, the legacy many of us seem to be leaving is the picture of a car, a family, a career, or a dream that has simply run out of gas and is now stranded on the side of a dead-end street. It's what happened (or is happening) between the opening narrative of our lives, "Once upon a time," and the closing-in-on-us scenes that have changed our perspective, leaving far too many people simply waiting for "The End."

I'm guessing there are things in life that each of us would like to change. We want the kind of change that ensures a better existence, both now and in the future. But, at this point, we may find ourselves thinking the existence of something—*anything*—better is only for story-time with innocent children. This is because we've become pirates of hope, robbing ourselves and those we love of any concept that involves the vibrant hues of a radiant sunset, ever glowing on our shoulders. If only *happily ever after* truly existed.

Mind-Space

At this point, I, you, *we* could merely cast off any personal responsibility with a simple, mitigating defense: *"C'est la vie."* If you don't recognize the phrase *C'est la vie* (pronounced se-lä-vē), it's a French idiom which means *"That's life"* or *"So is life."* In modern *American*, the verbal concept would be *"That's just the way it is"* or *"It is what it is"* or, even, *"Oh well."*

I've mimicked the disparaging essence of *C'est la vie* many times in my life. In fact, the thesaurus I used to have running through my head always seemed to say something like, *"This sucks. I can't change it. Screw it."*

BUT, had I known then what I know now, and had applied the inspiration God's already given us in Scripture, my vocabulary would have radically changed. The conversations I'd have with myself would be specific to the *"hopeful expectation"* and *"restful trust"* I now have welling up inside of me.

Really?

I didn't say *"every moment of every day."* In fact, as I write this, I just sent an email to someone confessing that *the Source of this book is my only source of hope*. What I mean by that is that *God's Sweet Spot* is the only source of hopeful and lasting fulfillment—even when I'm writing.

I had run into a bit of writer's block (if there really is such a thing) and was *"stuck"* (a concept you'll see often as you continue on this journey with me). My confession was that I simply needed to follow my own advice.

So I prayed. And, God guided me to add this chapter to the book. During the process of writing *"Learning To Live In God's Sweet Spot: From the Frustration of Running-on-Empty to the Fulfillment of Life Overflowing,"* each and every time I became confident in my own writing, I'd get stuck. Every time I thought I had it all together, a wrench would be thrown into the mix.

The only solution that ever seemed to work was relying on what I was learning *as I wrote*. As such, whenever I started to take a step outside of *God's Sweet Spot*, I began noticing it. And, I started recognizing each detouring and outward hike with much more clarity and swiftness.

That's why I entitled this chapter, "Selah-Vie." Instead of my old way of looking at things (that never seemed to work), what I needed more than anything in life was to rid myself of a "C'est la vie" mentality and invest myself in more of a "Selah-Vie" approach to every aspect of my life.

The word *Selah* is a Hebrew term that most Biblical scholars believe to be a musical expression, as it is used 71 times in the Old Testament *Book of Psalms* (meaning Book of *Songs*). A rough translation of Selah would be to *"take a break"* or to *"pause."* So, when Selah is intentionally written into a song/Psalm, it simply means to take a musical break or pause.

Perhaps the "pause" is written into many Psalms because it was a quiet break, intended for reflection. Reflection on what had been sung, instead of simply, quickly, and habitually moving on to the next verse. Or, in the case of many of us, reflection for the sake of avoiding the same mistakes we always seem to make.

For our purposes, throughout this book, we will be taking time to experience what I like to call *"Selah-Vie." Vie* meaning *life*. Yes, the phrase is a combination of both Hebrew and French. When taken at face value, Selah-Vie means to *"Pause for reflection on life."*

The change each and every one of us most desperately needs in life will require us to reflect on what we're experiencing right now, where we've been, how we keep getting there, and realizing the amazing truth that **God has a better plan for us**. Not only that, but that He is waiting for us to realize that we're running-on-empty and for us to open our mind-space to a better way.

Your "Vie"

The expectation you should have as you read and apply the simple principles found on the pages in front of you, is that your life will move beyond the kind of apathetic methodical existence that our culture revolves around. Instead, *your* world will become filled with *hopeful expectation*.

Take a moment to think that thought aloud. In this very moment, use your vocal chords and say to yourself, *"I have hopeful expectation for my life."*

No, really! If you want to see true and lasting change in your life, begin speaking positive affirmations over your past, current, and future circumstances. Right now, say aloud, ***"I have hopeful expectation for my life."***

As good as it may feel to visualize that kind of day-to-day existence, there's an even greater reward awaiting you. Mundane and ordinary days will be replaced by extraordinary and overflowing fulfillment. Instead of dreaded fear or exaggerated procrastination, you'll face each day with hope, excitement, and purpose. But that's still not the greatest reward.

The greatest reward will be the intimacy you build with God along the way. You will no longer fear because you will know what it truly means to trust in, cling to, and rely on Him—without hesitancy or doubt. You'll no longer put off change. Rather, you'll wholly embrace change, even when it comes with challenges. You will confidently lean on God instead of reactively relying on yourself. I believe the intimacy you'll build (or rebuild) with God as we journey through this process of change together will propel you into the reality of the sweetest kind of existence—one you've never even dared to whisper aloud.

The Transformation

How long will this transformation take? When will your *C'est la vie* become overwhelmingly positive, instead of overbearingly negative?

When can you expect to start seeing lasting changes in your attitude, outlook, and reality?

Your life will begin changing for the unequivocal best the moment you begin taking a reflective look on life, gleaning valuable information from your past, and intentionally choosing to put one foot in front of the other—one day at a time—constantly moving in a fulfilling, content, and trusting direction. Be assured that your journey will not only be filled with *hopeful expectation*, but will also provide you with the necessary tools to begin living every single day of the rest of your life in *restful confidence*.

You will embrace each moment with a peace that surpasses any human intellect. The unknown will never again be uncertain because you will fully trust every turn along life's journey to embody grace and goodness. This kind of peaceful trust eludes most people because they've never engaged in or experienced the refuge and strength found in *God's Sweet Spot*.

To get us there, we'll survey everything we study—from this point forward—with a reflection (Selah) on what we're learning and see how it applies to our lives (Vie). Though God is the only true source of lasting change, in order for the change to take place, we must be *active participants*. After all, that's not too much to ask if you want the fulfillment of your verbal affirmation, earlier: **"*I have hopeful expectation for my life.*"**

> "What are YOU going to do about it?
> ~ *Me, to my dad, at the age of seventeen*
> **...and now to YOU!**

Selah (Pause for Reflection)

Take 15 Minutes _and Make this Chapter_ Personal

> NOTE: Always keep a Bible, notebook, and pen ready. I believe God will open himself up to you during this time of reflection, just as He does for me.

Earlier, I asked you to verbalize what may be a new concept in your life. I asked that you declare, aloud, "I have hopeful expectation for my life." In order for this statement to become a reality in your life I want to add a *qualifier*. The additional phrasing may—or may not—be something you can fully embrace right now. Still, it's vitally important that you begin thinking and speaking words of hope and life—rather than destructive, self-fulfilling prophesies—over your present circumstances and future dreams.

Try these words on for size. Even if they don't fit your current mindspace, you'll find yourself growing into them as you journey forward:

> **"I have hopeful expectation for my life _because_ I have restful confidence in God's plan for my future."**

- Repeat that phrase, several times, out loud, right now.

- Commit to speaking those words every day for (at least) the next seven days, allowing the declaration to become your daily mantra.

  One thing I've found helpful is to set a reminder on my phone for a specific time each day that displays those exact encouraging words. And, each time my phone reminds me, I actually take time to read the phrase aloud and reflect on its promises.

I also like using index cards for this kind of thing. I write out the encouragement I need and keep the notecard in my pocket. That way I know I'll see it at some point in the day. And, when I do, I take the implications seriously.

As I mentioned, you may not always feel the hope of proclaiming fulfilment over your life, but read it aloud anyway. Why? Because the Bible encourages us to speak life—rather than death—over our lives.

> "*Death and life* are in the power of the tongue, And those who love it and indulge it will eat its fruit *and bear the consequences of their words*" (Proverbs 18:21, AMP; *emphases* mine).

So, if you just skimmed this "reflection" area, without making the declaration of faith over your present circumstances and future dreams, or without making a personal reminder to change your mind-space, please take a moment and do it now. It truly is THAT important!

Chapter Three

THE PATTERN PUZZLE: HOW THE STORY USUALLY UNFOLDS

"In qualitative terms, what one thing will you do today
that your future self will thank you for?"
~ *Daron Garmon, author*

More than *"once upon a time"* there still lives a person who has had some issues and that same person wants to take a walk with you, tell you a story or few, and see if you can relate. That person is me. I'm just a regular guy who's spent most of his life in either some kind of emotional turmoil or stuck in the laziest of ruts.

Sure, there have been good times along the way; but, I usually end up right back in the same old places. Until now, the best description of me would be that I am a person who has some regular (and some irregular) tendencies that have often left me feeling emotionally distraught, confused, or even angry. And this repeated pattern—more often than not—lands me in a place where I find myself feeling mentally and physically depleted. Most of the time, my annoying cycle also leaves me feeling spiritually distant from God.

That doesn't sound like a resume for success, especially if you're hoping to discover God's purpose for your life and learn to live inside the refuge of His absolute best. *Distraught, angry, confused, and distant* don't seem to align with a title that speaks of living in *"God's Sweet Spot."* But, I'd dare to say that feelings like these are common for many Christian believers.

That's why I'm putting myself out there—a personal unveiling—for anyone and everyone to see. I'm writing as a regular, everyday Christian to other Christians who find themselves living beneath (perhaps *far* beneath) the *"Sweet Spot"* kind of life that Jesus promised us when He said,

> "...I came that they may have and enjoy life, and have it in abundance [to the full, till it overflows]" (John 10:10b, AMP).

I have a message of hope for every single one of us that has the power to transform our lives from average to extraordinary. From half-empty (even totally running on fumes) to overflowing. The solution is a simple one, but it takes intentionality. The hope I'm offering you and the key to living an enjoyably overflowing life is to learn how to *cut your own personal cycle short*.

> ...The key to living an enjoyably overflowing life is to learn how to cut your own personal cycle short.

You see, most of us seem to spend way too much time recycling the same old scenarios and initiating worn out plays detailed in the pattern of our own outmoded handbooks. Over and over again, we repeat the same mistakes, often not realizing we're in a pattern until we've landed at the same, undesirable destination once again. But, when we learn to cut our personal cycle short, by altering our pattern, our otherwise preprogrammed destination will be *supernaturally* rerouted to a place of joy, contentment, and abundance.

That being said, I believe the sole source of life's overflow is God, and the best way to open the wellspring of God's beauty and goodness in our lives is to:

1) Learn from our past and the paths of others;

2) Learn how to alter our future by taking the guided trail God has already chosen for us—the pathway that will bring us (and Him) the most personal joy and fulfillment;

3) And, learn to be keenly aware of when we're choosing our own way rather than God's way (this one's not always a no-brainer).

As we replace our old, repeating patterns and the resulting flux of negativity that impacts our day-to-day lives with this new way of thinking, the darkness of our past will fade into the brilliance of God's perfect blueprint for life. That blueprint is outlined in story after story in the Bible. The Bible is also packed with pertinent directions for living the kind of life that most people only dream of. Sadly, most people have lost all motivation for dreaming anymore, let alone the pursuit of God's absolute best for their lives.

We're going to change all of that! The journey you've begun by reading this book—and the resulting application of God's principles—will lead you to the astounding realization that you don't have to dream anymore, because you will be living God's fulfilling vision, *each moment of every day!*

Let's take a look at an awesome promise in Proverbs 16:3. Most English translations of Proverbs 16:3 say something similar to *"Commit to the LORD whatever you do, and He will establish your plans"* (New International Version). That's a great promise, right? But how do I live it?

Throughout this book, I'm going to help you personalize similar verses until they take full bloom in your life. When God's written Word begins to blossom in ways that surpass hopeful expectation, they will also spring forth positive momentum in your garden of life.

Watch that same verse come to life as you take a look at it in the context of the preceding verse and by reading it in the Amplified Version of the Bible:

> "All the ways of a man are clean and innocent in his own eyes [and he may see nothing wrong with his actions], but the LORD weighs and examines the motives and intents [of the heart and knows the truth]. Commit your works to the LORD [submit and trust them to Him], and your plans will succeed [if you respond to His will and guidance]" (Proverbs 16:2-3, AMP).

Proverbs 16:2-3 are keys to opening the floodgates of God's blessings in our lives. Here's the way I'd sum up those same verses and tie them to the promise of overflowing joy in our lives: "By keeping our focus on God and completely relying on His direction, we'll be able to avoid misdirection, stay away from certain missteps in life, and end up in the best of all places: *God's Sweet Spot*—the place our hearts have longed for all along."

Believing you're reading this in hopes of learning a new and better way of living, in the next couple of chapters I'll be assigning names to some of our most common distractions, describing every detour in ways that make them personal to each of us.

These are not, however, mere lessons in futility. The things we'll discover together will become the catapulting steps that carry you to a place where you are ready, willing, and able to leap—with restful confidence—into an atmosphere where you were meant to soar.

Prepare Yourself

Along the way there will be an unearthing realization of just how we often get stuck in neutral—for way too long—along life's journey. Probably the biggest shocker will be the earnest and heartbreaking truth of how much of our lives we've spent distracted, detoured, and *stuck*—without even knowing it. But, once we name our distractions and assign some simple ways to stay on the right course, we'll be well on our way.

So, if you want to get from where you are now to a place of abundant and fulfilled living, the first thing on the agenda is to take an in-depth look at your current circumstances and make an honest assessment of how you keep ending up in the same (or similar) place time and time again. Once we take the time to analyze the *pattern puzzle* of our lives, we will begin to see a contrast between our current modus operandi and that of the true, personal happiness and contentment God desires for each of us. Then, for the remainder of this book, we'll learn how to take a few noninvasive—yet committed—steps which will enable us to solve the pattern puzzle of our lives and learn to consistently live in the sweet refuge of God's personal best. To start with, see if the story of how things used to be for me sounds familiar in your own life's commentary.

The Pattern of My Puzzle

Usually, for me, things seem to go well for a while. At least that's how I like to tell my story. It's important that you begin personalizing the belief that life is not always bad. In fact, life can be really good; especially when you discover and learn to live by a few key concepts that we'll be discussing throughout this book. For right now, however, let's continue our observation of how life often seems to go for many of us.

Things seem to go along well in my life for a while, though I never know how long those "good" times are going to last. Then, the inevitable happens. I hit a bump or two. Those bumps, however, are usually only a short detour or delay in the traffic pattern of my life before I find some sort of reprieve or seek some kind of temporary escape.

The bumps are difficult in the moment. Afterwards, however, I do what I usually do when one of life's difficulties has come and gone. Instead of being thankful to God for getting me through the circumstance, I find myself feeling vulnerable to further pain and decide to retreat.

I want life to be cozy, not bumpy. The path of least resistance is what I desire. But, the cozy, easy den I usually decide to rest in is not a place of refuge. It's a rut.

Due to my comfort, it takes a while for me to realize I'm in a rut. I'd compare my laxed stage to a well-worn couch that just seems to suck you in. The next thing I know, I'm eating chips, watching Netflix, and the indentation in the couch becomes my home.

Have you ever sat in the same position for too long? After a while, parts of you become numb and others become achy. As I consider both ramifications, even the numbness is achy. In the middle of my "comfortable" retreat (otherwise known as a rut), I find myself in a deeper pain—stump your toe in the middle of the night kind of pain. That pain is usually deeper than the bumps I was trying to avoid.

The pain I feel is often related to some sort of emotional, financial, or relational circumstance. More often than not, my pain—and the resulting internal and external conflict—is the product of a chronic and stinking way of thinking that has a way of repeatedly invading my cerebral space. I find myself slipping, sliding, or (even worse) jumping head-first into some messed up place or thought pattern. And I wonder, *"How'd I let myself get here?"* Life seemed to be going okay; but, now, everything seems so mixed up or messed up.

Sometimes my story even seems to replay itself. I really don't know how to explain it better than the idea of *déjà vu*. Right in the middle of playing my favorite song, my life-story seems to rewind and then begins playing the whole story over and over again. It's like my life is on a replay mode or loop of some kind. And the loop I find myself in *isn't* usually a reel of a sunny day at the park.

Déjà Vu

Let me tell you about a little déjà vu moment I had recently. This short tale was during a tumultuous time of my life when nothing seemed to be going right, even my phone wouldn't seem to charge. The story, in and of itself, isn't a life-changer. The chronicle does, however, assure me of one of the greatest game-changers in life: *Unless I begin to learn from my past, I'll keep replaying the same story.*

I rarely upgrade my phone to the latest and greatest. In fact, I often let my service carrier's contract expire for months on end because I know that—sooner or later—they will offer me a deal I can't refuse. As I write this, my contract is up on my service and I'm waiting for the first few attempts at offering me an upgrade to pass.

I know they can do better, and I'm waiting for the right deal. At the same time, I recently had an issue with my phone that caused me to believe I'd have to upgrade without *any* compelling deals on the table.

My phone would hold a charge, but the problem was in getting it to *take* a charge. Every time I plugged my phone in, I'd have to wiggle the wire, put the phone in some odd position, and hope for that "zong" sound that indicates I'm getting power to my phone. Then, I'd carefully move my hands away from the charger and slowly back away, only to see the lightning-bolt-shaped power indicator disappear and I'd have to start the whole tedious process again.

At first, I thought it might be the cheaper charging cables I was using instead of the proprietary ones the manufacturer suggests. And, since I bought all the cables (strategically placed throughout the house) at the same time, I thought perhaps I just needed to buy a few newer ones.

Instead of buying the three longer cords I was accustomed to using, I bought one proprietary cable and decided to see if it made any difference. *It didn't.* So, I started thinking (because they don't make phones to last anyway), maybe the port on my phone was loose and I could have that part replaced.

Before taking my phone to the repair shop, however, I decided to do an internet search for the problem. I typed in something like "loose charging port" and came up with multiple YouTube videos. I watched two or three, but nothing that seemed to be working for me. After watching what I thought was going to be my last instructional video, I was offered some, otherwise, related videos and one of them seemed totally different from the others; so, I clicked on it.

It was like I was watching an infomercial made just for me and the problem I was having. The guy described the same issues I was having to a "T."

Then the moment came when he offered a solution. The guy said that if I was accustomed to carrying my phone in my pocket, lint can often work itself into the port. *He then picked up a thumbtack and started scraping the inside of the port of his phone with the pointed end!*

What?! That seems a little too rudimentary. I mean, the idea of using a sharp object to scrape the inside of my phone doesn't seem technologically sound.

Still, I tried it. And, with each gentle scrape, a little ball of fuzz emerged from the charging port. Finally, when I was afraid any further poking might damage the phone, I plugged it in and immediately heard the "zong." Tada! No more problem; and, I didn't have to upgrade my phone yet!

It wasn't until the next day, proud of my accomplishment, that I remembered having this same issue with an older version of the same phone. And, here comes the *déjà vu* moment: I realized that when my older phone wouldn't charge, I had done the *exact same search*, seen the *exact same video* some years earlier, done the *exact same procedure* (on a broader port), and gotten the *exact same surprising result*!

I know. That sounds crazy; but, that's truly the way it happened. The thing is, "life in replay" happens to me all the time, *except* in more important areas of my life than the complications of staying electronically connected.

Back to Reality

Ugh! Now that the rabbit has been chased, and the dog has said *"squirrel,"* let's get back to the way things had been for me for way too long before I discovered what I believe to be the key to true happiness and contentment in life.

My story usually starts by taking a few steps in the right direction. Maybe even several leaps in the right direction. But then something happens, and then something else happens, and then I end up with a few too many steps in the wrong direction; or, I end up stuck in a rut of complacency. The rut is familiar and becomes easier and easier to live in; but, it's also a place where little to no progress is ever made.

As I've taken the time to examine my life and what often seems like inadvertent inconsistencies, I've actually noticed that I have a particular repeating pattern in my life that—unless the sequences are altered—I end up on replay, living the entire saga over and over again. The pattern I've discovered isn't simply that I keep making the same mistakes or ending up with little to no progress to show for my hard work. This pattern is much more subtle and seems to affect many Christian believers who find themselves doing more striving to simply exist than they do living and thriving with a dedicated purpose.

It seems to me that many of us have tendencies to replay pieces of our lives, repeat bad behaviors, continue making poor decisions, or repetitively and impulsively react rather than prayerfully and consciously respond to our situations and our relations. And, these things almost always recycle us back to a place of personal apathy or—worse—inward and outward intolerability.

What About You?

Have you ever noticed a repeating pattern in your life? Maybe it wasn't until just now that you even began to think about your life as a puzzle that has a distinctive pattern. One that if you could just figure out what the complete picture was supposed to look like, you would be able to make some specific alterations, put the pieces together, and solve the pattern puzzle.

Maybe you have a loop running through the continuum of your life's story that shows up in a day-to-day paralyzing notion of fear. Maybe dread or panicking fear is the big monster that keeps raising its nasty head and you've been immobilized and stuck for longer than you can even remember. Perhaps your independent nature (often just a tame way of saying *self-centeredness* or *pride*), has left you feeling all *too* alone in life. *Or,* you may be on the total opposite end of the spectrum. Instead of pride, maybe you are suffering from constant negative or demeaning thoughts about yourself that leave you full of doubt, insecurities, or even self-hate and loathing.

Maybe you have a pattern when it comes to personal relationships. Either you're apprehensive about being too interpersonal and transparent with anyone, you're all in with every relationship way too fast, you're jaded from past experiences and have become a "runner" when things get too serious, or maybe you're so distracted by getting your own needs met that you slowly deplete everyone around you and end up right back where you are now.

I know the patterns. I've lived with all of these puzzling patterns in my life. And the list goes on. How about depression or its close-cousin anxiety? For many people these are daily struggles, wearing us down and leaving us with a heightened sense of alarm or feelings of hopelessness.

Yet, as we look closer at any of the examples I've given, there's a pattern. You may not have realized it before. Heck, you might be in denial about it right now. *But, the pattern is still there.*

Do you struggle with contentment in your life? Never happy? Always searching for the next thing that will fill that immeasurable void? Perhaps you're constantly on the diet hamster-wheel, with your weight fluctuating up and down so much you can't even define "normal" bodyweight anymore. Why?

No matter your pattern or mine, there is a better place to live. We can give up that makeshift shanty we seem to come crawling back to and learn to make our permanent place of residence in *God's Sweet Spot*.

I Used To Be Controlled By Mine

The patterns that have repeatedly left me hunkered down in my own haphazard shanty have always seemed to run along the vein of self-centeredness, selfishness (yes those two are different), pride, and even addiction. But there is hope for us all!

As you delve into the simple solutions outlined in this book, I'll share some personal stories about my own patterns and the steps I've taken that have helped me defuse or shorten these destructive, repeating loops. These are also the same steps that have enabled me to learn how to live the richly overflowing kind of life Jesus promised us.

I have to say, as I reread that last paragraph, I must confess that there are still times when I find myself face-to-face with myself, challenging my status quo with what I know to be a better way. The great thing is that I've learned to shorten my stay in the shanty and make my home in the refuge of God's best for me.

If you truly want to live in *God's Sweet Spot*, take the challenge and walk with me into the best that God has to offer. To begin our journey, we're going to go a little further back in time than you might have expected. You see, for many millennia people have found themselves in the same place we often find ourselves: *in the same place*. So, please join me for a quick lesson in the history of our own humanity.

Selah (Pause for Reflection)

Take *15 Minutes* and Make this Chapter *Personal*

> *NOTE: Always keep a Bible, notebook, and pen ready. I believe God will open himself up to you during this time of reflection, just as He does for me.*

"Grace" is an odd term. It's used in so many ways in our modern culture. In essence, however, grace means giving someone something they haven't earned or that they don't deserve.

- Though God already knows every misconceived pattern in your life, He loves you enough to give you grace. Read and ponder the implications of this passage on your own life:

    "How can I know all the sins lurking in my heart? Cleanse me from these *hidden faults*. Keep your servant from deliberate sins! *Don't let them control me*. Then I will be free of guilt and innocent of great sin" (Psalm 19:12-13, NLT, *emphases* mine).

Perhaps you have already begun identifying patterns in your life that have previously been covered, masked, or are hidden faults. Maybe your repeating loops are even a deliberate means of self-inflated power or manipulation. Regardless, if you want to discover the refuge of *God's Sweet Spot*, it is of utmost importance that you begin your journey by asking God to clearly reveal your personal overt *and* covert patterns in ways that are deeply personal and uniquely discernable.

- Take a moment to pray Psalm 19:12-13 (the passage above) in your own words. As I consider my own, personal longing for a deeper, intimate relationship with God—the source of all true hope—I might pray something like,

> *"Father God, I don't always recognize my own, personal failings—emotionally, mentally, financially, strategically, relationally, or otherwise. Please impress upon my heart the often unnoticed patterns in my life that are keeping me from experiencing Your absolute best. I also know there are obvious repetitions in my behavior that urgently need transformation. I don't want to be controlled by my own imprudent ways. Instead, I desire to be guided and cleansed by living in the refuge of Your grace and presence. Please show me each of my unhealthy patterns and help me live the kind of life that is evident of peace, grace, and complete fulfillment. In Jesus' name I pray these things become true in my life; amen."*

You can know, beyond any shadow of a doubt, that God will hear and answer this kind of honest prayer, because His patience with you is filled with grace. Yes; God's grace is available, even to someone like you (and me).

Chapter Four

WHAT'S THE POINT OF A HISTORY LESSON?

*"Those who cannot learn from history
are doomed to repeat it."*
~ *George Santayana*[4]

I have personal rules for riding or driving in a car. The rules are: whoever is driving is also in control of the heat and air, decides whether windows are up or down, and determines what's listened to on the radio (if anything).

When I'm driving, I like to have fresh air seeping through the cabin; so, I almost always have a window cracked. I like to be warm in the winter and cool in the summer; so, I adjust the air accordingly. And, I like to keep the atmosphere of the vehicle positive; so, I listen to K-LOVE radio. K-LOVE is a nationwide (worldwide, if you listen on the internet) Christian radio station whose purpose and demeanor is defined by its tagline: "Positive and Encouraging."[5]

A woman I once worked with, and spent some time driving around with, made a comment to me one day while K-LOVE radio was playing in the background. The song playing was *"Dear Younger Me"* by the Christian group MercyMe.[6]

The song is a reflection on the artist's life and his desire to be able to write and deliver a letter about the ups and downs of life to a younger version of himself. He wishes that as a younger man he would have known God more deeply and understood God's graceful ways. The artist simply wishes that he knew then what he knows now.

The woman I was riding with, seemingly out of nowhere, burst into a ranting monologue about the theme of the song. She often listened to the same radio station and this song had really been bugging her. She went on and on—in various argumentative ways—ultimately saying, "This guy should just get over it!" She then asked, "Aren't we just supposed to get over the past and live for our future?"

That made sense to me. I might have made the suggestion that we live in the *present* instead of the future; but, it made sense. I mean, shouldn't we learn to just move on, despite our past or our present circumstances?

Later on that day, however, I began to really ponder her question. I started thinking: *This guy just wants to rewrite some of his own life's history.*

Some people may say that they wouldn't change anything in their lives because their past has made them into the person they are today. I get that. I, too, am much stronger because of the struggles I've faced, the obstacles I've had to overcome, and the wounds and scars that I carry from battles that have played out in my life. But, regardless of your background or current circumstances, there is at least a thing or two that many of us would like to rewrite concerning the accounts of our lives.

Rethinking

Over the next several days, I began to think about the term "history" and *why* we study the accounts of days, years, decades, scores, centuries, and even millennia of those who have gone before us. The *American Historical Society* gives us this insight as to the benefits of studying history:

> "When we study it [history] reasonably well, and so acquire some usable habits of mind, as well as some basic data about the forces that affect our own lives, we emerge with relevant skills and an enhanced capacity for informed citizenship, critical thinking, and simple awareness." ~ Historians.org[7]

In other words, we study history in order to gain insight into how *not* to make the same mistakes over and over again. Studying our past helps us make future decisions that will develop us into the kind of people who are useful to ourselves and helpful to our fellow man. *I* would *exclamatorily* add that it also helps us make positive movement in the direction God best desires for our lives, which then puts the rest of our story into a right perspective.

The Future of Our History

Repeating the same old patterns just doesn't make sense. *We can't keep doing the same things, expecting different results*. The answer, however, isn't simply making better decisions or in doing things differently this time around. Those things will work for almost anyone, at least for a season. But "a season" just isn't enough to tilt life from running-on-fumes to life overflowing.

I want more than an extended spell of what *feels* like happiness. From what I've experienced, those highs only last for a while anyway. And, the end result of that forward momentum you *were* feeling is that those highs often come to an abrupt halt when a series of difficulties come your way.

We need more than a bandage here. We need healing. I want true, lasting contentment in life. I want to rest in the kind of refuge where I believe—no matter what's going on—God loves me and desires what's best for me. I want to trust God so much that I begin to see all of life as beautiful.

Can you say that right now? Can you say, *"I am content with my life. I know God loves me and desires what's best for me. I fully trust God and His purposes for my life. I have begun to see my life and the world around me as beautiful"*?

Perhaps you're not able to *convincingly* say those words right now. That's okay. Because I believe you will find those exact words dripping—even flowing—from your lips by the time you complete this book, *if* you consider and put into practice the concepts that are outlined. In fact, right now would be a good time to write those words—in your own handwriting—inside the back cover of this book. And sign it. Go ahead and do it:

> "I am content with my life. I know God loves me and desires what's best for me. I fully trust God and His purposes for my life. I have begun to see my life and the world around me as beautiful."

Then, read those same words aloud.

Doesn't it feel good to say those words? Just wait until you genuinely begin tasting the sweetness of those prophesies as they come out of your mouth and become your life's mantra.

Step by Step

The first step toward this kind of healing, peace, and contentment is to realize we have a particular pattern puzzle that continues to loop us back to the same (or similar) places. The second step is to define that pattern. Only then can we truly solve the puzzle by learning to cut short our cyclical tendencies and return to God's best plan and purpose for our lives—*God's Sweet Spot*.

❖ ***Where It All Began***

Usually, for most Christian believers, we start in the sweetest of places. Our journey begins the very day we decide to place our trust in Jesus Christ's life, teachings, death, and resurrection.

Jesus came with a purpose and a promise for all of us. His purpose was (and is) to open the doors of heaven to us so we can live in infinite intimacy with our Creator. He came to offer himself as a sacrificial scapegoat for all of our rebellious ways and make us right with God by taking the punishment for our sins upon Himself. And, the promise He gave us is an eternal home in heaven—a place where there will be no tears, no death, no sorrow, and no pain (see Revelation 21:4).

But that's not the only promise Jesus made. Jesus also promised us His peace, His help, and to enable us to live the best kind of life anyone could dream of: *abundant and overflowing*. Some of us have taken Jesus up on the offer of forgiving our sins, but we've been conditioned to believe that an abundant and overflowing life is *only how fairytales end*.

As we get started on the path to a place that is inconceivably grander than our wildest dreams, consider what your journey was like when you took that very first step. Let's say you have placed your faith in Christ to forgive you of your sins and make a home for you in heaven. Do you remember what you felt like when you first made that decision?

Maybe your heart throbbed all the way up and into your throat! You just knew you had to *go for it*. That's the way it was for me as a young child. It was the first time I'd ever heard an explanation I could understand about God's unconditional love for me, His acceptance of me, and the lengths He'd gone to just to be able to hold me in His arms forever. WOW!

I couldn't wait for the preacher to get to the part where he asked people who wanted to accept God's love, grace, forgiveness, and hope— as a Gift from God Himself—to come to the front. I knew the pattern of the service and knew the "invitation" part was coming soon!

My dad and I walked the isle to the preacher and accepted God's invitation and gift to each of us, together. We also got baptized together. It was a time and a feeling I'll never forget.

What a feeling!

It's also the same feeling I get when my relationship with God is at its closest. When I'm seeking to grow in my relationship with Him. When I want nothing more than to rest in His sweet refuge. It's the feeling I get when I'm in *God's Sweet Spot* and know that I just have to *keep going for it*.

To me, living in *God's Sweet Spot* and "going for it," means that I'm living in a state-of-mind where whatever God wants is also what I want. And *that* feels good. There are many words to describe this kind of feeling. You may call it peace. Others may call it awe. Some may even call it thrilling. I simply call it *"the fulfillment of life overflowing."*

That state-of-mind—and whatever word or phrase you've related to it—also has an associated action word (verb). The related verb is called *Trust*. And *Trust*, by definition, is always active and growing.

However you describe your feeling, that feeling also has a place (noun) associated with it. And that noun is **also** called *Trust*. It's a residence we can take up and live in.

This kind of *Trust* is where we'll begin our pattern discovery and learn the, otherwise, repeating *future of our history*. As we walk through this loop of life, we'll begin our journey by reflecting on the place we want to be and live: In an active, unfaltering, "go for it" kind of Trusting relationship with God, because this truly is "God's Sweet Spot."

History Repeats Itself (Ugh)

One might consider that if we'd ever experienced this kind of *Trust*, we'd never want to leave it. Sadly, from the place called Trust, the next place we usually settle is in a place called *Complacency*. This is most often the second design in our pattern, which is then followed by the schematics of *Frustration, Independence, Rebellion, Trouble, Surrender, Rescue*, and then (sooner or later) we come full-circle back into a *Trusting* relationship with God again.

A difficulty, however, arises when we consider each of these phases. Though they often manifest themselves in a sequential order, they don't have to. For example, I can quickly jump from *Trust* to *Complacency* to *Independence* without ever sensing any real *Frustration*.

Because of this, we may never even realize that we've abandoned the refuge of God's absolute best. As such, it is key that we define each of these phases and reflect on them as they relate to the *pattern puzzle* of our own lives. All the while, however, don't forget this key concept:

> Wherever you are in the pattern, it's possible to cut your cycle short and get to the place called "Trust" once again.

Let's Get Personal

To illustrate these age-old patterns in our own lives, I'll be putting a personalized voice to our pattern. I'll be giving you a behind the scenes look into my story. In my narrative, you'll learn the intricacies of how I've found myself in a pattern of Trust, Complacency, Frustration, Independence, Rebellion, Trouble, Surrender, Rescue, and Trusting again.

> Wherever you are in the pattern, it's possible to cut your cycle short and get to the place called "Trust," once again.

It's the story of mankind, really. For as long as people like you and me have walked this earth, we—just as generation after generation of people, throughout time and through the Bible—repeat the same old patterns, over and over again. Though many of the Biblical accounts of these patterns would have been the *headline news* of the day, they have become so redundantly repetitive in our own, every-day lives, we hardly even notice them.

A few highlights of the Biblical headlines that elude us today come from Deuteronomy, chapters 30-32, Psalm, chapter 78, and Nehemiah, chapter 9. When you recognize yourself *in my story—or* theirs—please know that there's hope, even for those who might otherwise feel *hopeless*.

Selah (Pause for Reflection)

Take *15 Minutes* and Make this Chapter *Personal*

> *NOTE: Always keep a Bible, notebook, and pen ready. I believe God will open himself up to you during this time of reflection, just as He does for me.*

As you take a "pause" and reflect, please find an easier-to-read translation of the Bible (there are tons of them online). I prefer my regular reading out of something that flows with modern English; so, I use the New Living Translation (NLT). I keep the NLT, the New International Version (NIV) and the English Standard Versions (ESV) handy at different places around my house.

- If you're easing your way into this process—which is a good way to start—begin by finding a New Living Translation (NLT) of the Bible (easily found at Bible.com or BibleGateway.com);

- Read the entire chapter of Psalm 78. It may seem a bit long, but you'll see why this is a great way to discover true life change;

- Be sure and make notations on which verses the Israelites were either in a state of Trust, Complacency, Frustration, Independence, Rebellion, Trouble, Surrender, Rescue, or Trusting again;

- Take five minutes and write a short list of any tendencies where you see any variation of these same repeating occurrences in your own life: Trust, Complacency, Frustration, Independence, Rebellion, Trouble, Surrender, Rescue, and Trusting again;

- Then, pray the essence of Ephesians 3:16 over your own life. Pray it for a week, every day, and look for the changes that begin to take place:

"Father God, I pray that from the depths of Your glorious and unlimited resources, You will empower me—deep within—with the kind of inner strength that only You can provide. Through Your Holy Spirit, I pray you lift me up, prepare me, and strengthen me for everything ahead of me today. In Jesus' name I ask these things; amen."

Chapter Five

IN _____ WE TRUST

"It takes two to tango—the one who risks (the trustor) and the one who is trustworthy (the trustee); each must play their role."
~ Charles H. Green, The Trusted Advisor[8]

Each time I've ever heard the phrase, "It takes two to tango," the first thing I think is that the couple mentioned are likely to need counseling—at the least—maybe even mediation. I'm sure the *Tango* is meant to be romantic and enticing. But, usually when the term is used with that kind of phraseology, it means there's a major malfunction in the dance of entanglement.

I remember one of the times I decided I was going to do something different in a relationship. I didn't want to *Tango* any longer. I wanted to *Salsa* or, at least, do *"The Ballroom Blitz"* (The Sweet, 1973). This compulsion to change things, in particular, was with my *third* wife.

Our marriage was on the rocks. I didn't know what to do. I knew our emotions and hearts were hemorrhaging and hoped I could find a tourniquet to—somehow, hopefully—slow the bleeding. I began a frantic search for some way to spend time with my wife and with God at the same time. I knew that's what she wanted. And, I knew it was definitely what I *needed*.

I bought a book that is the basis for an email devotional I still receive to this day. I can always identify which emails I need to read because they're from someone I know or expect. This particular email always reveals the sender as "Loving Actions." And who, in whatever mind-state, doesn't want *loving actions*—both given and received—to be an incremental theme throughout their lives? The *Loving Actions*[9] email newsletter always contains an excerpt from a book by Gary and Norma Smalley called, of all things, "It Takes Two to Tango."

I bought the book with an earnest desire to mend a relationship, *but, unfortunately, never invested the energy to read it*. There were many books I read, counselors I sought, and changes I made *after* my third wife had been drained dry. My efforts were the epitome of *too little, too late*. In hindsight, there are so many things I wish I would have taken the time to learn. Things I wish I would have done differently. Even things I simply wish I'd never done or said.

When the Song Remains the Same

In Chapter One, I mentioned being on "an extended stay with God." These stints were few and far between for quite a while. But, when they came, I found momentary peace.

According to my own *predictable* patterns, I'd choose God's way for a while. Afterwards, however, I'd be enticed into a comfortable rut by my own insecurities.

After my third marriage was laid out on the mortuary's cold, hard table was one of those times when I desperately sought God. I was broken, felt beat-down, and I was dreadfully confused. But, I was seeking God. Crying out. Begging for help.

In the craziest of all places to ever predict an encounter with God—especially at my level of emptiness—I was cleaning a dirty bathtub when I felt a sense of calm come over me that was quite peculiar.

I realize this kind of thing doesn't happen to everyone, but I felt like I heard God audibly speak to me. What I heard (at least in the reverberation of my head and the consciousness of my heart) was God saying, *"If you give up control of what happens to this broken marriage and hand the reins over to Me, I will attend to your current separation and the two of you will remain one. If, however, you choose to keep your meddling hands in the situation—trying to control the outcome yourself—I will take My hands out of the circumstance and you'll bear the consequences."*

Do you know what I did? I did what every person who's in desperate need of God's intervention does:

> I waited two days (maybe it was only a day) before becoming impatient with "God's timing" and decided He must need my help in getting things done! Yes; I put my meddling hands where they didn't belong.

Hanging

If you've been in a place of impatience with God, His timing, or completely living independent of His leading, you already know the answer to the title of this chapter. It might not be the answer all the time. It might not even be your answer most of the time. Or, maybe it's your reaction more times than you'd like to admit. But, the answer that keeps landing you in a hollowing rut is: "In <u>ME</u> I Trust."

God takes too long. And, who knows if He's going to do what I asked Him (like a genie in a bottle) to do? Right?! Have you ever been there?

As I write, there's a hand-painted sign hanging over a doorway just fifteen feet away from the comfort of my writing space. The artwork is of a dramatic sunset over a body of the darkest blue water. Clouds are sparse, as are the few birds flying off into the sunset.

That's the way the picture started. And, it's the way I originally wanted it to end. But, evidently there's this thing embraced as "artistic license" when it comes to individuality and its interpretation.

Even now, as I sit with hopeful expectation, I see the wisdom of an artist's heart. The added caption is a one-word-wonder, added just minutes before the painting was handed over to me. In ALL-CAPS, striking the face of this beautiful sun-laden array is the word "WAIT."

It gets even better than that. The word "WAIT" has an ellipsis (...) following it. And that's a good thing!

Every day I gaze into the eyes of this reminder. It's a memoir of what it truly means to Trust God. For me, the sunrise *and* sunset is eclipsed by the restfully confident *"wait."*

That's what genuine *Trust* is. It's being restfully confident, even in the *hanging,* waiting moments. Simply put, it's an inner peace that is indescribably, yet perfectly real.

> [Jesus said] "I give you peace, the kind of peace only I can give. It isn't like the peace this world can give. So don't be worried or afraid" (John 14:27, Contemporary English Version).

This is the kind of peace and restful confidence that leaves us in awe. Maybe you've been there before. Perhaps God stepped into a tumultuous time in your life, made Himself real, and you found yourself—at least momentarily—in *God's Sweet Spot*. You felt good about life, love, circumstances, even your future. You were absolutely sure—this time— you'd find a way to actually reside in this place of trust and refuge.

What happened? Are you still there? If not, maybe the realization of a repeating pattern in your life is becoming real as you read these accounts of my turmoil.

What is God's Sweet Spot?

Perhaps you've missed it thus far, but the place of actively living in Trust **is** *God's Sweet Spot.* It is the only place you'll find contentment, joy, and life overflowing. Trusting the God of the Bible brings with it so many promises. Promises offered by the One True God, who is incapable of breaking His Word.

In the "Selah" section of the previous chapter, (I hope) you read Psalm 78 and made notes according to the history of the people of the Bible and noticed some of the same patterns in your own life. Another great example of our seemingly complicated pattern puzzle is found in Deuteronomy 30. The structure of our lives is the same as the Israelites; we just have more options for where (or in whom) we place our Trust.

> "...the LORD your God shall make you abundantly prosperous *in everything that you do*, in the offspring of your body and in the offspring of your cattle and in the produce of your land; for the LORD will again delight over you for good, just as He delighted over your fathers, *if* you listen to *and* obey the voice of the LORD your God to keep His commandments and His statutes which are

written in this Book of the Law, and *if* you turn to the LORD your God with all your heart and with all your soul (your entire being)" (Deuteronomy 30:9-10, AMP; **emphasis mine**).

Jesus, Himself, said that the greatest commandment in the entire Bible is to love God with all of our heart, mind, soul and strength (see Mark 12:30). In other words, you have a singular purpose for as long as you have breath in your lungs. You are to love God. And, the only way to truly love someone is to Trust that person (with all of our heart, soul, mind, and strength).

The promise is emphatic. And, God is morally inept of even the thought of breaking His promises. *If* you make a conscious decision to seek God, learn to trust Him, *and* consequently fall in love with Him, *you will see* the fulfillment of His promises in your life. It's truly that simple and simply that *sweet*.

Learn and Live

According to John 14:27, mentioned in the "Hanging" section above, Jesus offers each of us an active Trust. A living Trust. He offers us a secret place to dwell with Him, day-to-today and moment-by-moment in perfect peaceful Trust.

If the kind of peace Jesus is offering you isn't the kind of peaceful trust you have during your current circumstances—if this isn't the restful confidence you're feeling in the reoccurring pattern that keeps evading your happiness—*please know* that it can be. Learning to have and then live in *Trust* is a bottom-line theme you'll see repeated throughout this book.

Trust is a verb and a noun. Learning to live there is what you're doing, right now. But, living in that active place can often feel illusive.

Are you restfully confident about everything in life right now? *About anything?*

I simply encourage you to keep reading. There are things we still need to embrace about ourselves. Patterns that we need to engage. You didn't get to a place of frustration and emptiness overnight. Usually the pattern is quite deceptive and we rarely know we're being drawn away from God's simple, yet profound, best.

The first step we usually take in the wrong direction is the easiest. I've already given this step a name. Do you remember it? Consider what it means when you say, "I'm good to go."

Selah (Pause for Reflection)

Take *15 Minutes* and Make this Chapter *Personal*

> *NOTE: Always keep a Bible, notebook, and pen ready.*
> ***Why?*** *I believe God will open himself up to you during this time of reflection, just as He does for me.*

As you take a "pause" and reflect, please consider whether you could find peace and unfaltering reliance in these circumstances:

> "…We were under great pressure, far beyond our ability to endure, so that we despaired of life itself. Indeed, we felt we had received the sentence of death. But this happened that we might not rely on ourselves but on God, who raises the dead. He **has delivered us** from such a deadly peril, and *he **will deliver us*** again. On him we have set our hope that *he **will continue to deliver us*** (2 Corinthians 1:8c-10, NIV; **emphases mine**).

Past, present, and future. That's where Trust is held and where *God's Sweet Spot* resides. As you ponder that profound reality, write a list of anything that pops into your mind—from one to a thousand—of times when:

- You know your life was inexplicably altered for the good;

- You feel your life was assaulted by changes that didn't make sense;

- You can—in hindsight—see a correlation between the two;

- Nothing makes sense of your circumstances at the time;

- In each of these moments—you were truly trusting God OR were trying to manipulate Him with your pleas for help.

If you made your lists, contemplatively praying the paraphrased fulfillment of 2 Corinthians 1:8-10 will help free you from the patterns that besiege you:

> *"Father God, things may not always be easy. In fact, they often seem like more than I can handle. BUT, I am choosing—in this moment—to believe that You've always been there for me. Not always in ways that I would have chosen, but I'm still here and I'm doing my best to be hopeful in the midst of my circumstances. Please help me to trust in, cling to, and rely on the strength You are offering me, even now, and for my future."*

Chapter Six

GOOD TO GO

"Don't give up what you truly want for what you want right now."
~ *Daron Garmon, author*

When I first got married, we tried to make sure every detail was in order for the wedding. Catering. Flowers. The church. We didn't want our guests waiting too long after the service, so we were strategic in planning when the photographer would take pictures. Everything was planned. Premarital counseling, where we'd go on our honeymoon, even how much weight we wanted to lose in order to look our best in pictures.

Okay. That last part—losing weight—wasn't even on my radar. But, it was definitely in the forefront of my bride-to-be's mind.

She wanted *this day* to be the most special of any day she would ever experience in the realm of her entire life. And, to fully enjoy *her day*, she wanted to feel comfortably beautiful in her wedding dress.

Of course I never mentioned anything closely related to weight—as that is a forbidden territory *for any man*. But, since she was losing a few pounds, I decided I should too.

We both lost down to weights we hadn't seen on a scale since our pubescent years. In fact, looking back on our wedding pictures, I think we went a bit overboard.

The crazy thing about marriage, however, is that it has a tendency to *grow* on people. I know this isn't true for everyone, but for many of us—men and women alike—we have a tendency to gain weight after marriage.

For women, it can often be because of childbirth. But, I've also seen the same phenomenon take place when *no* children were added to the fold. *And*, marriage isn't always the qualifier either. In fact, I've witnessed the fleshing out of a couple when they'd simply dated for an extended period. Haven't you?

Trust me. I know I'm ruffling some feathers. But, we all know this *weighted* trend to be true—at least for *someone else*.

Poundage didn't happen to us overnight. In fact, I remember a time in our earliest years of marriage when a teenage girl in a youth group we lead said to my wife, "You remind me of Barbie." (How presh?!)

But, it wasn't long before we became a bit too comfortable in our stretching skin. She was great at baking and I've always been a reasonably good cook. Add to the equation the fact that we both *love* to eat.

Even when she wasn't baking and I wasn't cooking, I remember times when we'd order an extra-large pizza, twenty-four battered hot wings, sit in front of the television, and eat the whole enchilada in one sitting. Of course, I ate most of it. And, it began to show.

I think I must have weighed around 175 pounds—fully dressed—when we got married. Years later, I knew I'd gained some weight, but didn't realize how much. I had a few guy friends who were also uncomfortable with their post-marriage weight gain. So, collectively we decided to do something about it. As an incentive we decided to make a bet to see who could lose the most weight in 90 days. I think we each kicked in forty dollars (as a side-note, money is always a motivator for losing weight).

When we weighed in for the initial plumb-line documentation, I had maxed out at 242 pounds. I'd gained almost seventy pounds since getting married! All because I became *comfortable*.

The SAME Story is in the Bible

In today's society, there is much emphasis on being politically correct; but, in the days when the Bible was written, there weren't any such rules. Being "fat" was called out with poignancy. There were no uncertain words. And the Bible's accounts of such plumping were not segregated by men or women. Not by race, origin, age, abilities, or inabilities. In fact, there was a whole group of people—God's people—who simply got comfortable, lazy, *and* fat.

This was a people who once found themselves in a trustful, reliant, all-consuming, personal relationship with God—the lover of their souls. However, coexisting with this reassuring existence was an obsession with *comfort*. As such, these people's reliance on God became less and less intent. They became more dependent on themselves than anything else.

Have you ever been there? In a place where your relationship with God began to wane simply because you became too comfortable?

These people—who had been wooed and wowed by God through His provision, His sheltering defense, and His unwavering dedication to their well-being—had simply, yet profoundly, lost touch with their sole provider. They no longer talked to God about everything, relying on Him in every circumstance. Instead, they moved about their day with *minimalized* reflection on God, if any consideration at all.

Talking to God had become something they fit in or, perhaps, never even thought about in the midst of their "stressed out" day. And, *they didn't even notice the change.* God's provision, protection, and outpouring of grace were just humming noises in the background of their existence.

I am fortunate to have a washer and dryer in my home. I realize many people don't. Both machines are just a few feet away from where I spend most of my time writing, relaxing, eating, and enjoying everyday life at home. But, I've become so accustomed to the sound of my dryer running that I don't even hear it anymore.

It's there. It's humming. But I don't notice it. In fact, I never even hear the buzzer when the dryer has stopped. It's gotten to the point where I have to leave a light on in the laundry room to remind me that I have clothes to fold. Even then, I'm often oblivious to the light.

During the timeframe of the following passage, God's best was playing in high definition, right in the midst of the people who should have heard the consistent humming of His love. But, they could no longer hear it. They weren't even able to hear the buzzer as the dryer stopped running. They were fattened by their contented living.

Take a moment to truly ponder the kinds of things God does for His people—the "wow-factor" of following and Trusting God. Then take a look at how many of us—like the Israelites—begin to plump up:

> "For the people of Israel belong to the Lord; Jacob is his special possession. *He found them in a desert land, in an empty, howling wasteland.* He surrounded them

and watched over them; he guarded them as he would guard his own eyes. Like an eagle that rouses her chicks and hovers over her young, so he spread his wings to take them up and carried them safely on his pinions. The LORD alone guided them; they followed no foreign gods. He let them ride over the highlands and feast on the crops of the fields. He nourished them with honey from the rock and olive oil from the stony ground. He fed them yogurt from the herd and milk from the flock, together with the fat of lambs. He gave them choice rams from Bashan, and goats, together with the choicest wheat. You drank the finest wine, made from the juice of grapes" (Deuteronomy 32:9-14, NLT, *emphasis mine*).

The first thing that jumped out at me when I read that passage was not the great provision of God, but the place of disparity He brought His people out of. The Bible says that the people of God were in an "empty, howling wasteland." That's not a place you want to be. But, that's where I found myself before I discovered the Truths of the chronicles I'm sharing through the pages of this book.

Empty. Howling. Think about the term "howling" for a moment. When does a wild animal howl? And, if you've ever been camping and heard that howl, how did it make you feel? Add, on top of all of that, the concept of living in your most imaginative understanding of a "wasteland."

I don't know what you've been through in life, but my gut wrenches when I think of the emptiness I've felt. In relationships. When it comes to finances. When it comes to feeling insecure about my future—even my present.

I know what it means to feel the hairs on my neck stand straight up when I sense the *howling* of uncertainty or danger in my life's circumstances. I know what it means to dread the night and, at the same time, hope I will go to sleep and *never* wake up.

My "wasteland" may be different from yours, but I've experienced the kind of hopelessness that seems like quicksand—slowly dragging me into a pit of despair. I know the inhospitable surroundings of loneliness. I know the wasteland of abandonment. I know the wilderness of living each day, hoping for the best, yet experiencing the worst. I know what it means to collapse beneath another day of exhausted nothingness.

❖ ***But God...***

The Bible says that God rescued His people from this negativity and turmoil and gave them good and gracious things. It says He surrounded them, guarded them, and watched over them.

I can't even fathom honey flowing from rocks or extra virgin olive oil oozing from gravel. Yes; I know that's not what actually happened. But, the verbiage describes an affectionate and miraculous exhibition of God's provision. Re-read the passage (Deuteronomy 32:9-14) again and try to imagine each of God's elaborate gifts. The agricultural implications may seem a bit abstract, but try to imagine having everything you need—with plenty left over for your wants. Can you picture what that would look like in your current circumstances?

Toddler Time!

Have you ever had one of those "Thank You, God" moments that truly wowed you in the very instant it happened? Then—with the attention span of a toddler—forgotten how fortunate you were to have been a part of one of God's timely miracles in your life?

Sometimes the blessing is obvious and we celebrate it in the moment, only to let our minds wander anxiously to our next perceived need. Other times, we don't even hear the dryer running and are oblivious to the blessing altogether.

Have you ever been running late for work (or some other appointment) and passed the wreckage of a horrible accident? I have. As I finally weaved my way through the mess and traffic began moving again, instead of thanking God I was running late—realizing that I could have been in that tangled mess if I hadn't been running behind—I looked at the clock on my dashboard and sped up in an effort to make up for lost time. These are the times when our dryers are humming; but, we don't hear a thing.

Another example of deafness to God's provision and care is when we feel like we've made our own way. Have you ever discounted things like these as coincidences, a making of your own effort, or just "good luck" instead of God's loving care?

- You received an unexpected bonus at work;

- The rental agent at your apartment building gave you a few days grace;

- You passed an officer of the law—parked in the medium of a fast-paced highway—going way over the legal limit and didn't get pulled (when you know you deserved it);

- A test came back from the doctor's lab that was *surprisingly* good;

- Money to pay *that* bill became available, seemingly out of nowhere;

- A tumultuous time your pubescent teen was going through seemed to work itself out;

- The right thing happened at the right time and you landed on the right side of the fence—where the grass was actually greener (and the water bill wasn't higher).

❖ God Who?

The verse immediately following God's deliverance of His people from a barren wasteland into a place of complete fulfillment—where they were dedicated to and Trusting Him alone—says that they forgot all about God in the midst of their comfort:

> "But Israel soon became *fat and unruly; the people grew heavy, plump, and stuffed*! Then they abandoned the God who had made them; *they made light* of the Rock of their salvation" (Deuteronomy 32:15, NLT, *emphases mine*).

What just happened?!

The New Living Translation of the Bible says that the people of God became so comfortable and confident in their "own" successes that they "made light" of their relationship with their sole (soul) provider. The same thing has happened to me and I have a hunch it's happened to you as well.

When I first started writing this book, God gave me idea after idea. He helped me structure the process of how things should flow. He flooded my head with thoughts and my composition book with notes. I felt like things were being downloaded so fast that I would knock this book out in a month or two, send it to a few friends, and a whirlwind of changed lives would quickly ensue.

What actually happened was I got caught up in the spin cycle again. As I reflect on how the cyclone began, I realize it started when my *head* became *fat*.

At first, I wrote every day. I wrote for hours at a time. Words flowed faster than I could type. That's when I decided I needed to start promoting the book. I felt like the book would be finished soon and that I needed to begin promoting it. All the publishing gurus say promoting your work is as important as writing it. Following their *expert* lead, I felt like I had to do what would be best for the book's success. That's when my mind began spinning out of control. I was obsessed with researching ways to promote this promising new book.

I never even noticed, but as my head became wrapped around all the online tutorials, books, and courses on writing and publishing, I started writing less and less. After a while of getting nowhere with the promotion of the book, I simply stopped writing.

In the midst of *self*-promotion, I forgot my original purpose. I forgot about promoting God and the influence He wanted to make with the inspiration He'd given me. Somewhere along the way, I'd "made light" of God and my time with Him. My head got fat, and I forgot my God.

Complacency Unraveled

Notice that Deuteronomy 32:10 says that Israel was found in a "desert land." That's exactly where you and I are bound for (again) if we become Complacent and don't realize we're growing *"heavy, plumped and stuffed."*

When I gained that seventy pounds, I didn't even notice. Sure, I had to buy bigger clothes and my energy level was slightly depleted. But, I could still put on some fancy clothes, do my hair just right, and look like a superstar.

That's exactly where the Israelites found themselves. They were superstars! But "they made light" of the One who'd given them their fame and fortune.

As I sit, writing this book, I just quit a job God has used to sustain me for many years. To most people (myself included), it may seem crazy to leave a provisional position to write a book and *expectantly hope* for God to make a way. But, that's what I've done. I'm tired of being *too* comfortable.

Have you gotten there yet? Are you too comfortable?

Maybe you're not comfortable at all. Perhaps that's because you've progressed past Complacency and moved on to another stage. Maybe you're like me and are in a constant spin cycle of Trust, Complacency, Frustration, Independence, Rebellion, Trouble, Surrender, Rescue, and Trusting again.

Eventually the spinning cycle causes the washing machine to get frustrated and it starts banging, bumping, and even displacing itself on your laundry room floor. Don't worry. God has an answer for that too!

God has an incredibly satisfying plan for your life. It's called Trust. And the result is living in the "secret place" of *God's Sweet Spot*. There is, however a conundrum when trying to get to that place of fulfilment.

If you desire to live outside of the frustration of *running-on-empty* and want to find your way to the *fulfillment of life overflowing,* you—too—have a part to play in the manuscript of your life. You see, as I study Scripture and am getting to know God better, I've found this ONE crazy thing to be true: Outside of God's initial advancement of creation, each and every miracle chronicled in the Bible, thereafter, required human participation.

In the beginning, God said, "Let there be…" and it was. Afterwards, God said, "Let there be…" and then He required our participation through Trust.

Take RESPONSIBILITY While You're Waiting On God To Move!

Yes, I said it! God says it too! Take Responsibility!

I have a handcrafted painting on the wall of the vanity area of my bathroom. It quotes Jeremiah 29:11, *"For I know the plans I have for you,"* declares the Lord, *"plans to prosper you and not to harm you, plans to give you hope and a future"* (NIV). This verse is one that many people hold dear. It's a promise they like to believe will be their fortune in life. I often claim this promise for my own life. Who wouldn't?

But most people don't read the promise in context. At the time when God spoke this promise to His people, they had totally forsaken Him and were living in complete rebellion. The preceding verse says the consequences of the people's rebellion would be tough, but that God still loved them and would bring them through it.

There are consequences for our actions. There are even consequences for our inaction or Complacency. Though God didn't promise to erase the consequences of His people's rebellion, He did promise to rescue them. He even told them when He'd rescue them and fulfill His promise. The answer to when God's promise would come to fruition and the people would live in abundance, once again, is found in the verses that follow:

> "In those days when you pray, I will listen. If you look for me wholeheartedly, you will find me. I will be found by you," says the Lord. "I will end your captivity and restore your fortunes" (Jeremiah 29:12-14, NLT.)

The same promise God made to the Israelites is true for your life. God loves you so much that He wants to see you through every life circumstance. He desires to help you—even rescue you. He wants to give you a hope for your future. If you find yourself in a place of Complacency, you don't have to stay there. Determine today that you will shorten your spin cycle by doing your part—praying and seeking God with all of your heart, especially when you don't feel like it or don't feel like you need it!

Selah (Pause for Reflection)

Take *15 Minutes* and Make this Chapter *Personal*

> *NOTE: Always keep a Bible, notebook, and pen ready.*
> ***Why?*** *I believe God will open himself up to you during this time of reflection, just as He does for me.*

Perhaps you know you've been Complacent in your relationship with God. Maybe you know you're a little further down the rabbit hole and have crossed over into Frustration with Him, Independence from Him, Rebellion against Him, or are in outright Trouble. Either way, don't beat yourself up. Instead, learn to recognize where you are and cut your cycle short.

Throughout this book, we'll be learning more about our tendencies and how to find our way into God's "secret place" of complete fulfillment in life. In the meantime, find solace in knowing that God already knows your patterns, and He loves you anyway:

> "Because of the Lord's great love we are not consumed, for his compassions never fail. They are new every morning; great is your faithfulness" (Lamentations 3:22-23, NIV).

God loves you. He is compassionate toward you. His mercies are new every morning. And He is faithful to His promises. All you have to do is participate and receive!

To help make this chapter more personal, take ten minutes—right now—to get on your knees (if you're physically able) and pray. As you pray, tell God you need Him. Tell Him you've been doing life your own way for far too long. Tell Him you want to live for Him. Tell Him you don't know how to seek Him with your whole heart. Ask Him to teach you. Tell Him you love Him and thank Him for His love, mercy, and compassion. If you think you've run out of things to say, just tell Him those same things over and over again. The key is to truly spend intimate time with God and let Him do the rest.

Then, do this same thing, every day, for the next seven days. I'm guessing you'll begin to see a difference in the hope that IS your life's future.

Chapter Seven

IF GOD REALLY CARED ABOUT ME

"The only disability in life is a bad attitude."
~ Scott Hamilton, Olympic Gold Medalist[10]

In a conversation with a friend, I asked her how her recent vacation had gone. I was *not* ready for her response.

She'd told me she was going on vacation several weeks earlier. I'd asked her where she was going and what she had planned. But, in reality, I didn't listen to anything more than the fact she was going to South Africa.

It was pleasantry, watercooler conversation. I was glad she was able to take a vacation, but I tuned out when she started giving details.

I know that sounds mean, but I wasn't going. *She* was. I haven't been on a *real* vacation, ever. So, her words went in one ear and out the other when she was telling me about the *exciting* trip she was about to take.

A few weeks after her announcement, I asked how her escape had gone. She immediately went into storytelling mode. I became an audience for the abundance of joy that came from her trip. She said that this planned break had become the greatest thing she's ever done.

To my amazement, this woman had not taken a trip to South Africa to trace her genealogical roots or to see one of the seven natural wonders of Africa—Victoria Falls. Though she did see the falls—and was in awe by them—what she wanted to tell me about was her *safari* adventures.

Minute after minute, I saw pictures and heard tales of her riding an elephant and the pictures of others in her group riding elephants. She showed me pictures of zebras, hippos, rhinoceroses, giraffes, lions, and even the carcass of a zebra that had been killed by a lion and then scavenged by hyenas. All of these pictures were taken on her phone, including selfies with lions just meters behind her.

I love nature and was excited to see her pictures of the falls, but am not sure I would have wanted to endure the heat and ferocity of a safari. However, there were two wilderness expedition pictures she showed me that were awestriking.

The first was of a five-something in the morning sunrise through the branches of a single tree. I have a certain affinity for trees and for sunsets. Though this was a sunrise, this picture was worthy of *National Geographic* magazine. It is the kind of image I'd get up before 5 o'clock in the morning to see—every day.

The other picture was of a giraffe, head cradled downward into a local water source. This picture was taken on a smart phone but should be on the front of a *Hallmark* card. As the giraffe was taking a life-giving drink from the still water, this woman's camera also captured the giraffe's reflection in the water beneath its stooped and elongated neck.

After a while, however, I was tired of seeing pictures and started feeling uneasy about listening to her great adventure. She sensed my frustration and said she had things to do and would let me get back to what I was doing.

As she walked away I muttered, *"Thank you. I don't want to see any more of your pictures anyway. I'm so glad you got to go on vacation, but I'll never see anything like that. How is it that some people get all the breaks in life and I just struggle to get by?"*

She didn't hear me, but I did. And I knew God did. Immediately my frustration was revealed to me as jealousy—what the Bible calls *coveting*. My gut wrenched. Why was I so frustrated, instead of excited? The next words out of my mouth—still speaking under my breath—were: *"God, I'm sorry. I should be happy for her, but the reason I'm not is because I'm frustrated with my own life circumstances. Please help me be content. You have always provided for me. Thank you, Lord."*

But it didn't end there. I had confessed my fault, but it was only lip service due to a guilty conscience.

That evening, I stewed over the fact that a fantastical vacation may never be mine. I begrudged the fact that so many of the people I knew were living lives of luxury, all while working from home. Other people got to go have lunch with their kids at school in the middle of the day, while I had to scrounge for any and all work I could find just to eek by.

This wasn't just a covetous, jealousy thing. It was an anger thing. I was angry with God. How could so many people have it so good, go on vacations several times a year, buy new luxury automobiles, shop half of the day, live on the lake, have nannies, dog-sitters, housekeepers, lawn maintenance guys, and have their groceries delivered? All the while, I was the one hoping to get the job delivering their groceries!

I was beyond frustrated. And, here's an important detail that you need to know: God had recently delivered me from a mountain of debt. He'd used an unfortunate circumstance to pay off my mound of credit card debt, had relieved me from my car payment, and left me with a better vehicle than I had before—paid in full.

And here I was, blaming God that I had a "pauper's" lot in life.

❖ The Phone Call

Ever since the thought of writing this book became a part of my reality, I have prayed for God's inspiration. I've asked that this book be His words and not my own. As such, I pray about what God wants me to say and what stories will best represent His purposes.

Several days prior to my interaction with this kind woman, who just wanted to share her joy, I had been praying for God to reveal a story that would convey the "Frustration" portion of life's spin cycle. There were two or three stories I was pondering, but I knew they weren't the right ones. Then God opened my eyes to what I call my "safari blues." This story illustrated everything He wanted me to express. Anger, Frustration, blaming God, giving Him lip service of remorse, and forgetting all He'd recently done for me.

Still, the story had some gaps. The greatest chasm was that I needed to truly repent and get back to a place of sweet joy in God's everyday provision. But, I also knew I had to make a phone call.

I called this wonderful woman and asked if she'd be willing to give me some personal information. She asked what I wanted to know. I know you're never supposed to ask a woman's age, but I did. She told me her grandchildren had tried to bribe her into revealing her age and that she'd always resisted. She told me nobody knew her age, and that she didn't plan to tell me. She did, however, offer me a loophole when she asked *why* I wanted to know.

I told her about our recent encounter and how it had made me feel. She indicated that she could sense that I was uneasy and that was why she'd cut her show-and-tell story short.

I apologized for what I was feeling, how I had acted, and told her that I needed to get back to the *Sweet Spot* of God. I explained that complete Trust was where I needed to be, but that I was stuck in a place called Frustration.

As we talked, she told me that things hadn't always been easy for her. That she'd often struggled as a single mother and had experienced many trying times in her life. We talked about Trust, Contentment, and Frustration. We also talked about how God has always made a way for each of us. Then, we talked about the book you're now reading.

I asked if she'd be willing to read the first six chapters and give me some feedback. I told her I'd mention her in the book and that one day people would read about how God impacted my life through her. She declined any mention of her name. But—to my total surprise—she did tell me her age and gave me permission to share. As I sit and write this chapter on Frustration, my safari loving friend is 73-years-old.

God used this spirited, mature woman to cut my spin cycle short. And, though I am perfectly content with the fact that I've never seen Victoria Falls in person, I am certain I'll see true paradise one day.

The Root of Frustration

When my life is lacking in the area of intentional intimacy with God, instead of God's sweetness, I focus on circumstantial sourness. It's during these times I notice I get agitated about the smallest of things. I get overwhelmed by things I can't control. I question. I doubt. Negativity becomes my norm.

When, however, I take the time to analyze my life from a temperate mindset and assess where I am in my own personal spin cycle of Trusting God, I am able to quickly reset and move from an unbalanced state of Frustration into the kind of peace which the Bible refers to as transcending understanding:

> "Do not be anxious *or* worried about anything, but in everything [every circumstance and situation] by prayer and petition with thanksgiving, continue to make your [specific] requests known to God. And the peace of God [that peace which reassures the heart, that peace] which transcends all understanding, [that peace which] stands guard over your hearts and your minds in Christ Jesus [is yours]" (Philippians 4:6-7, AMP).

The kind of peace the Bible speaks of requires some duty on our part. We pray, continue to pray, and we do the things God is leading us to do through prayer. But the peace that comes is a gift from God. It's a gift that comes from Trusting God—no matter our current circumstances—and believing He always has our best interests at heart.

Frustration, however, comes when we become Complacent in our prayerful, intimate, and Trusting relationship with God. Our Complacency quickly morphs our thoughts and our personal peace. Soon, our disposition becomes that of Frustration with life and circumstances. Often, we just assume the worst about everything and everyone—even God. We begin questioning God, blaming God, and even lying to God. Our prayers become lip service and our hearts become hard.

As you'll recall from the previous chapter, God had provided for every need the Israelites ever had. He had protected them and given them victory after victory over their enemies. But, they became content and Complacent in their intimate pursuit of God. And, as such, God allowed them to suffer the consequences of their actions. But, instead of cutting their cycle of Rebellion short, they began to blame God for their self-inflicted circumstances.

The Bible says that God continued to be merciful to the Israelites, even in the midst of their merited consequences. Though they weren't deserving, time and time again God miraculously provided for His people because of His unfailing love for them. Even so, the Bible records the grumblings of His people:

> "Yet they kept on sinning against him, rebelling against the Most High in the desert. They stubbornly tested God in their hearts, demanding the foods they craved. They even spoke against God himself, saying, 'God can't give us food in the wilderness. Yes, he can strike a rock so water gushes out, but he can't give his people bread and meat'" (Psalm 78:17-20, NLT).

Can you imagine how much it must have panged God's heart as these ungrateful people questioned Him and His ability and willingness to provide a stubborn people with things they didn't deserve? But, God is gracious. He is merciful. And He provides—even when we don't deserve it. As such, do you know what God did next? He caused the heavens to open up and it began raining grain. The Bible calls the grain "manna" and also refers to it as the "bread of angels" (see Psalm 78:23-25). The people now had a supernatural resource for sustenance.

The story gets even better. The people had demanded meat too. So, God caused a cyclonic wind to swirl, gathering an abundance of birds.

These winds then swept the birds right into the people's camp. There were so many birds collected that the people were able to eat the meat of this miraculous provision until the Bible says they were "gorged" (see Psalm 78:26-29). And do you know what their response was?

> "Then they remembered that God was their rock, that God Most High was their redeemer. But all they gave him was lip service; they lied to him with their tongues. Their hearts were not loyal to him. They did not keep his covenant" (Psalm 78:35-37, NLT).

The Israelites did exactly what I often do. They experienced God's provision and gave Him a nod of the head. But that was it! They immediately became Complacent to the point of simply giving Him lip service instead of honoring Him with their whole hearts. Then, they jumped right back into their destructive spin cycle.

Did you notice the indication of this passage that says "they lied to him with their tongues"? This is the part where they began blaming God again. They blamed God the very next time something didn't go the way they expected. The *lying* part is simply a way of saying they went about life, blaming God—out of Frustration—instead of taking responsibility for their own rebellious actions.

If you take time to truly absorb the story of the Israelites in the Bible, you'll see they have the same spin cycle as you and I. Their cycle revolves around Trust, Complacency, Frustration, Independence, Rebellion, Trouble, Surrender, and then Trust again.

If you were to draw a line on a piece of paper and the line represented a continuum between Frustration and agitation with life and that of true peace and Trust—with Frustration on one side of the continuum and Trust on the polar opposite side—where do you land most days?

Are you agitated, frustrated, and negative about life? Or, are you content, joyful, and swimming in the still waters of peace?

The key is to recognize your current spiritual state and cut the cycle short. *God's Sweet Spot* is the only place we'll ever find true contentment and discover the *fulfillment of life overflowing*. That place is Trust. Cutting short the cycle of Frustration can only be found in returning to a place of daily—minute-by-minute—wholehearted intimacy with God. The fruit of that intimacy is Trust rather than Frustration.

One way to move from Frustration, back into the *Sweet Spot* of Trust is to make a list of all the ways God has come through for you in situations you originally deemed as hopeless or frustrating. No matter where you are, there is a worse place you could be. And, no matter where you are today, there is a better place you can be. Focusing on either is unhealthy for our spirits and our minds. Instead, talk to God about everything and Trust that His plans for you are better than what you're currently experiencing. Know that God is gracious, even when you are wandering or wondering. Peace, rather than Frustration, comes when we Trust God, no matter what. Sadly, however, many people allow their Frustration with life, circumstances, and with God to lead them to the next place in the spin cycle of life: Independence.

Selah (Pause for Reflection)

Take *15 Minutes* and Make this Chapter *Personal*

> *NOTE: Always keep a Bible, notebook, and pen ready.* ***Why?*** *I believe God will open himself up to you during this time of reflection, just as He does for me.*

- Take a moment to write down ten things that are bringing you frustration in life right now. This list should be contrived of things that bother you on a day-to-day basis;

- Next, write a description of why you are frustrated about each thing/circumstance;

- As a third step, describe a time when you had a similar circumstantial frustration to each of the ones you've listed and described. In your description, note how each circumstance was resolved;

- As a turning point in this mindful exercise, thank God for how He's always been there for you, even if things didn't turn out as you'd hoped;

- Finally, consider how your intentional intimacy with God reflects your level of Frustration and why, using this verse as motivation to return to a life of sweet, intimate Trust:

    "Guard your heart above all else, for it determines the course of your life" (Proverbs 4:23, NLT).

Chapter Eight

HERE I GO AGAIN ON MY OWN

> *"It is our own arrogance and pride that cause pain.
> The more that we think that we can do anything,
> the less we realize our complete dependence on God,
> and the worse the pain becomes."*
> ~ Reshad Field, author[11]

There have been times in my life when an opportunity presented itself and it just made sense to move forward in that direction. These were usually times when a decision needed to be made and one of the paths seemed clearer; so, I made my choice and moved on. I didn't consult God. I simply took the course that felt right to me.

At times my gut decision was because God moved me in that direction, despite my lack of consult. Other times, things didn't work out so well. Then there were also occasions when I consulted God, discerned His best, and still chose to do things my way. I'm sure you can guess the outcome of my *Independent* choices.

❖ ***Blessings With No Prayer***

When I think about times in my life when I've taken a specific course of action—without consulting God—and things turned out for the best, I think about my relationship with my daughter. I consider a specific decision I never prayed about, but the outcome was the result of God leading me—even though I never thought about praying through the situation.

Across the course of several years, I built and destroyed relationships with people that my daughter cherished with her whole heart. Two people in particular brought joy, peace, excitement, and love into my daughter's heart like no one other than immediate family could ever bring. But, because my daughter knew these precious people were no longer in her life because of how she'd witnessed me treating them, she lost all trust in me. She'd seen arguments and knew that the relationships were broken because I didn't treasure these people the way I should. The way *she* did.

I would dare say my daughter even became fearful of me. Not that I'd physically harm her, but that I'd done things that had left her feeling vulnerable and hurt.

As such, she didn't want to see me. If she did see me, it had to be on her own (mom's) turf. She didn't want to come over for weekend stays anymore. She didn't even want to go out for lunch with me without her mom's presence.

I expressed my sincere angst about my daughter's changes to her mom. The response I received was that it had taken years to tear down the trust my daughter once had, and that it would take a while to get it back. In fact, the words her mom used when explaining my daughter's feelings was that I needed to *woo* her back into a loving, trusting relationship. She reassured me that my daughter loved me dearly, but that she just didn't trust me anymore.

Those were hard words to hear. And, my immediate thought was, "I don't care. Legally she *has* to spend time with me!" But, the more I thought things through, the more her mom's words made sense; so, I began the process of *wooing* my daughter.

I never prayed about any of this—though I should have. But, the end result is God wanted me to slow down, not involve the legal system—thus making things worse—and simply demonstrate to my daughter she could trust me again.

That's a perfect example of needing to pray, not praying, making an Independent decision, and it being God's perfect course of action. But, sometimes things don't work out so well.

❖ **Detriment Without Prayer**

Though there are more drastic stories I could tell, a broader understanding of how Independence can be detrimental would be when, as an early adult, I purchased a plot of land on the Broad River in North Carolina. The land was wooded in areas, had some towering black walnut trees throughout the property, a great open space for building, and an amazing expanse that was waterfront. I received owner financing and purchased the lot for $15,000. I often visited the property, took friends there, and had ideas of one day owning a home there. I, however, did not have the finances to develop the property. Still, I figured I'd hang onto it until I did.

Shortly thereafter, I married for the first time. We both had jobs, a place to stay, and circumstances seemed fairly stable during that time of our lives. We didn't really need the money, but I thought I'd put the property up for sale and see if we could make a profit.

We did! After only owning the land for a year and a half, we made a substantial $10,000 return. The buyers planned on converting the undeveloped land into a vacation campground. That sounded wonderful to me—and so did the extra cash in my pocket.

No less than a year and a half later, I decided to visit the property, see what they'd done, and find out its current worth. To no surprise, they'd done exactly what they said they were going to do. They had developed a fully functional campground.

Though very little had been done in the way of landscaping, they had built an office, a game room, activity center, and added shower facilities. However, the big kick in the tail was when I investigated the properties current value. It had increased from the selling point of $25,000 to a market value of $250,000. That was almost 25 years ago from the time of the writing of this book.

We didn't *need* the money. I *wanted* it. Still to this day I have no idea where the money went. All because I didn't stop and pray and discern if selling that property was God's will or my Independent nature. For the record, I don't even want to know what that property is worth now!

❖ **Prayer With An Independent Response**

Whatever your circumstances, the answers inspired and chronicled in this work will help you overcome your personal emptiness and find fulfillment in *God's Sweet Spot*. Most of my narratives are personal to me and have an underlying theme that includes my addictive nature. I pray you'll be able to transfer the concepts to your own life circumstances and find the hope that I have. This story digs deep into the demons that haunted me for way too many years:

After years of praying to win the lottery and promising God I would use some of the proceeds to commit myself to an addiction rehabilitation center, I finally gave up all hope of winning the lottery. I decided I had to take the chance of humiliation before my peers, as well as the financial disruption my decision would cause, and reach out for help. This commitment did not come without much prayer. I prayed and prayed and prayed some more. Every answer I received from God was, "Just trust me."

So, I did.

Between detoxing in a hospital bed and rehabilitating in another facility, I spent forty days and forty nights trying to get myself in order. I prayed every day, read the Bible every day, and spent time researching other Christian counsel.

As the days progressed, I began to believe I had this *addiction thing* under control. In the back of my mind I thought, "I've come this far, maybe alcohol really doesn't have a death grip on me."

To congratulate myself, on the evening of the day of my release from rehab I got falling-down drunk. The next day, I regretted my actions, but still had alcohol left in the half-gallon bottle I'd purchased. So, I decided I'd put myself to the test and try to portion my daily drinking.

That worked for about four days. Then it was on! I was right back to where I was before I went to rehab, drinking at least a fifth of straight liquor a day.

I remember the day my drinking finally got to me. I had a 7:15am appointment with my primary care doctor to check my blood pressure, adjust any medications, and have some lab work done. When I arrived at the doctor's office I checked in—as usual—using the palm-scan method. I was also asked for my insurance card, as they were updating their system (don't they say that every time you visit the doctor?).

I know where my insurance card is. It's in the same place in my wallet that it always is. But my head suddenly became foggy. I fumbled through my wallet several times before the receptionist finally said I could just have a seat and that she'd get the information later.

As I turned toward the exact same seat I always wait to be called from, I fell out. If you don't know that means, I passed out and hit the floor like a bowling ball dropped from six feet in the air onto a thinly carpeted floor.

When I came to, two doctors and three nurses were hovering over me. My primary doctor asked what hospital I wanted to go to. My Independent, Rebellious nature said, "I'm not going to the hospital." At which time my primary doctor said, "Let's get him to a room." They lifted me into a wheelchair and that's all I remember. I was *out* again!

By the time I came to, the next thing I remember was having my primary doctor's fingers jammed into where my carotid artery is. I also looked around and saw firemen and EMT personnel already there. By this time I had no choice but to go to the hospital.

Evidently, by the time they were even able to get a pulse and physical blood pressure reading, my systolic (upper number) reading was no greater than 70 and my diastolic (bottom number) reading was barely 60. This is compared to my normally—medicated—reading of 145/93.

I almost died. But, do you know what I did when I was finally discharged from the hospital for severe dehydration due to the abuse of alcohol? I went home and drank some more.

The next day, I was dizzy, nauseous, even convulsing to the point where I had to lay down and call for *more* help. I had prayed for God's help, He'd sustained me financially during my detox and rehab period, and everyone was proud of me for seeking help. Yet, I chose my own, Independent, way; and, things didn't turn out the way I'd planned or prayed. All because I chose to do things my own way.

Making the Correlation

When our life's washing machine reaches a certain level in its spin cycle, it seems uncertain that we'll be able to open the door and add a softener to the mix. Has that ever happened to you? When the washing machine wouldn't open because it was already in a certain state?

According to the progression of the cycle, there are times when it seems we can't open the door. It's as though the door is locked. In our current mindset, we can't figure out how to open the door and change the cycle or throw another option into the mix.

Sadly, it seems that many of us live life in the same way we set our clothes washer. We set it according to our desires and walk away. We never consider there may be a better option. We don't realize that, even though the door seems to be locked, there's always a way of resetting things. Why? Because when we're stuck in a particular stage of our cycle and we usually don't even recognize we're there. We've become *Independent*.

> "But they and our fathers acted presumptuously and stiffened their necks, and did not heed Your commandments. They refused to obey, nor were they mindful of Your wonders and miracles which You did among them…" (Nehemiah 9:16-17a, AMPC).

Have you ever been there? Are you there right now?

It's like we keep doing the same things—operating in the same patterns—and can't seem to figure out why we aren't getting any better? We've seen, lived, and experienced better; but, we keep finding ourselves in the same place.

It's a spin cycle Albert Einstein would call insanity: "Doing the same thing over and over again and expecting different results." It's hard to swallow the pill, but could you or I be "insane"?

We go about life, believing we know what's best for our lives. Yet, the same things our Independent nature tells us are *right* keep landing us in the *same* rut of the *same* spin cycle that keeps leading us to the *same* results. Here are a few verses to consider:

- "In those days there was no king in Israel. Everyone did what was right in his own eyes" (Judges 21:25, ESV).

- "A person may think their own ways are right, but the Lord weighs the heart" (Proverbs 21:2, NIV).

- "Enter through the narrow gate. For wide is the gate and broad is the road that leads to destruction, and many enter through it. But small is the gate and narrow the road that leads to life, and only a few find it" (Matthew 7:13-14, NIV).

In the first verse, we can clearly see that people did what they thought was best, without any Godly leadership. In the second, we see that we often think our way is right, but that God is the true judge of right and wrong. And, in the third passage, we recognize that going our way—though easier—lands us in the worst of all destinations.

Independence can be doing our own thing, simply because it's what we want or what we think is right. Simply put, Independence can be defined by doing our own thing without asking God about which direction to take or by simply choosing not to heed the advice He gives. Where do you fall most days?

Perhaps, when we're instructed to "pray about everything" (see Philippians 4:6 NLT), the advice is more than a suggestion. OR, you can keep doing things the way you've always done them, hoping—somehow—for a completely different result.

The spinning stage of Independence is often hard to determine because you're doing your own thing and don't realize you've fallen into the same old pattern. Try something NEW today and PRAY before you do anything else!

Selah (Pause for Reflection)

Take *15 Minutes* and Make this Chapter *Personal*

> *NOTE: Always keep a Bible, notebook, and pen ready.* ***Why?*** *I believe God will open himself up to you during this time of reflection, just as He does for me.*

Take a moment to:

- Make a list of all the things that concern you, worry you, that take precedence in your thoughts. Make special note of those things you know you're making Independent decisions about;
- Pray about each thing on your list;
- Then pray again;
- Pray a third time;
- Pray about these same things over the next seven days (at least) three times a day;

Then, claim the rhetorical question at the end of this passage as a personal promise:

> "Don't bargain with God. Be direct. Ask for what you need. This isn't a cat-and-mouse, hide-and-seek game we're in. If your child asks for bread, do you trick him with sawdust? If he asks for fish, do you scare him with a live snake on his plate? As bad as you are, you wouldn't think of such a thing. You're at least decent to your own children. So don't you think the God who conceived you in love will be even better?" (Matthew 7:7-11, The Message).

-

Chapter Nine

BULL IN A CHINA SHOP

"It is a difficult thing—if not impossible—to forgive oneself for foolish errors, not for trampling a life or goring another with sharp horns, but for being the fool who opened the gate and let the bull out, blind to potential consequences."
~ Richelle E. Goodrich, author[12]

When was the last time you used words as a weapon? You know: the kind of words that cut to the marrow of your opposition's spirit? How recently have you slandered another person to make yourself look better? How about the last time you lied? Took something that wasn't yours, but justified it? How long has it been since you took things a step too far—no matter your flavor of weakness, temptation, or upheaval?

No one wants to admit it, but we all have our weaknesses. Those places we go, things we do, say, think, or daydream about that are in complete opposition to God's best for our lives.

Not that everything has to be that drastic; but, we all do things that appear to be in our best interest. We engage in things that distance us from God's best plan for our lives. Sometimes these actions or attitudes are intentional. Other times, our actions are a result of habit or lack of self-control.

When we allow ourselves to move from a place of complete dependency and Trust in God into a Complacent realm, we open the door to Frustration, Independence, and—eventually—Rebellion. As I mentioned, it's not always intentional; but, the slippery slope is often hard to discern when we're in the midst of critical life circumstances and decisions.

When we've traversed this far along the rut-digging spin cycle of life, we often have thoughts of remorse, but rarely choose a different way. It's like the rut has been so ingrained that it's the natural progression we take—even when we don't want to. For many of us, the mechanical setting on our spin cycle of Frustration leads us straight into Rebellion. In this case the difference between Independence and Rebellion is often indistinguishable.

Have You Ever?

Have you ever hoped for something, didn't see things work out as you'd liked, gotten so Frustrated that you started doing your own thing, and found yourself in a pattern of self-destruction? I have. I've been there, done that, got the T-shirt, wore the T-shirt out, and have a whole closet filled with Rebellion-torn shirts.

> "But they put God to the test and rebelled against the Most High; they did not keep his statutes. Like their ancestors they were disloyal and faithless, as unreliable as a faulty bow" (Psalm 78:56-57, NIV).

The Classical Amplified Version renders "faulty bow" as: "...they were twisted like a warped and deceitful bow [that will not respond to the archer's aim]." It's during these times of Rebelliousness that God's purposes for our lives are most threatened. Although God is always at work, bringing good out of even the most destructive of circumstances or actions (see Genesis 50:20 and Romans 8:28), our Rebellion can often detour us from our greatest purposes and rob us of blessings.

God has a purpose for your life. A plan that is good. But those good plans are often missed out on because our Rebellion makes it impossible to hit the bullseye of God's best laid plans because we refuse to respond to His aim for our lives.

Though the Israelites' Rebellion was that of increasing wickedness, Rebellion against God isn't always defined by such starkness. Sometimes we defy God willingly. Other times our Rebellion can be subtle.

For instance, right after my first wife and I separated, I felt betrayed by God. I felt like He could have saved my marriage.

In retrospect, I destroyed my marriage. God put more effort into my marriage than I *ever* did. I had been living a Complacent, Frustrated, Independent life for way too long. But, at the time, I felt like my eventual divorce was God's fault. So, I Rebelled!

My Rebellion was of a stark nature. I became a womanizer, even philandering with married women. I drank, drugged, and defiled myself in ways I can't even begin to describe in these pages.

On the other hand, I've also Rebelled in more subtle ways. This book should have been completed six months ago. However, there have been days when I chose not to write and days when my writing was so limited that only a paragraph or two would get written. I'd always think, I'll just write more tomorrow. Or, in many cases, my own selfish desires would take priority over what I knew God had purposed me to do and I didn't write for days on end.

Recently, I felt deeply convicted by what I read during my morning devotion:

> "Now listen, you who say, 'Today or tomorrow we will go to this or that city, spend a year there, carry on business and make money.' Why, you do not even know what will happen tomorrow. What is your life? You are a mist that appears for a little while and then vanishes. Instead, you ought to say, 'If it is the Lord's will, we will live and do this or that.' As it is, you boast in your arrogant schemes. All such boasting is evil. If anyone, then, knows the good they ought to do and doesn't do it, it is sin for them" (James 4:13-17, NIV).

I felt convicted because I keep saying, "I'll write tomorrow." But I don't know what tomorrow holds. All I know is that God's will is for me to write this book and get it out to the masses so lives can be changed. Lives like yours. Like mine. And, if I don't write, it is a sin because I'm not doing what I am supposed to do. It's Rebellion. And my purpose in life is thwarted.

I don't know what your Rebellion looks like. It's likely that if you're in the midst of it, you don't know either. What I am absolutely sure of is that the enemy of our souls—the devil—wants to keep us depleted and keep us from enjoying the *Sweet Spot* kind of living God has in store for us. One that is ours for the taking if we'll simply return to a committed and Trusting relationship with the one true lover of our souls.

When speaking on this same subject, Jesus refers to the devil as a thief when He says:

> "The thief's purpose is to steal and kill and destroy. My [Jesus's] purpose is to give them a rich and satisfying life" (John 10:10, NLT, [bracketed] note mine).

What has the devil stolen from you because of your own spin cycle of Rebellion? A job? An opportunity? A marriage? A family relationship? Your dignity? Your health? Your wealth?

All of your emptiness can end in an instant if you choose to cut your cycle short and purposely pursue intimacy with God each and every moment of every day. The "rich and satisfying life" is not a fairytale if you truly seek it with all of your heart.

As Pastor Perry Noble says, "Today, may the shackles of shame be shattered as we realize what we did is NOT who we are! May we not allow shame to hold us in a prison of our own past and not allow us to see the potential of our future! Shame has caused far too many to suffer for far too long! Jesus didn't just die to take away our sin—but to take our shame away as well."

Selah (Pause for Reflection)

Take *15 Minutes* and Make this Chapter *Personal*

> *NOTE: Always keep a Bible, notebook, and pen ready.* **Why?** *I believe God will open himself up to you during this time of reflection, just as He does for me.*

For the next three days—no less than three times a day—pray the following Scriptures and ask God to reveal to you the ways you are Rebelling against Him and to give you glimpses of what He has in store for you when you decide to commit yourself fully to Him:

> "Keep your servant from deliberate sins! Don't let them control me. Then I will be free of guilt and innocent of great sin" (Psalm 19:13, NLT).

> "You will keep in perfect and constant peace the one whose mind is steadfast [that is, committed and focused on You—in both inclination and character], Because he trusts and takes refuge in You [with hope and confident expectation]" (Isaiah 26:3, AMP).

Chapter Ten

CAN LIFE GET ANY WORSE?

*"Whenever you look back and say 'if,' you know you're in trouble.
There is no such thing as 'if'.
The only thing that matters is what really happened."*
~ D.J MacHale, filmmaker/author[13]

I often say I have a face for radio. In truth, I have a voice for radio. My voice is strong, commanding, and recognizable after just one vocal encounter. As long as someone has heard my voice at least once over the phone, I usually don't have to identify myself when I call again.

I also have very distinct voice inflections. These articulations are something I've had to learn how to tame, especially as it pertains to my daughter—as I am still wooing her back into my life. I rarely have to raise my voice; my inflections say it all. A perfect example is when it comes to my cat, Occhio.

I can say stop, no, or quit doing that a hundred times and she just acts like she can't hear me. If you've ever had a cat, you know what I mean. But, when I raise my voice and change my inflection, she knows I mean serious business about tearing up my curtains, my shoestrings, my earbuds, or demolishing my daughter's dress-up clothes, make-up, and playtime wigs.

Whether it's a raised voice, a change in inflections, or—like when I was a kid—you heard your first and middle names all at once, you know there's Trouble brewing. When I heard "Daron Stephen," I knew I better find an alibi!

In today's world, nobody uses my middle name. But, I still know when I'm in Trouble.

Complacent Rebellion

Have you ever prayed a prayer that goes something like, "God, if you'll get me out of this" or "If you'll change this situation"? The prayer usually ends with some bargaining mechanism where we promise God something He knows we won't live up to.

The Israelites were—all too often—in Trouble. Real Trouble. The Bible chronicles everything from slavery, to famine, to the utter slaughtering of God's people. All because they became Complacent, Frustrated, Independent, and wickedly Rebellious.

Independence, Rebellion, and Trouble often go hand in hand. Trouble is usually birthed when we become Complacent; but, it isn't usually manifested until we've reached a place of Independence and Rebellion.

Nehemiah, Chapter 9—in its entirety—is a great synopsis of the Israelites repetitively spinning cycle, but verse 28 gives us a condensed summation of how things transpired:

> "But as soon as they were at rest, they again did what was evil in your sight. Then you abandoned them to

the hand of their enemies so that they ruled over them. And when they cried out to you again, you heard from heaven, and in your compassion you delivered them time after time" (Nehemiah 9:28, NIV).

As soon as the people became Complacent, their cycle began again. And, each time their Independence and Rebellion landed them in a place of Trouble. In this case, Trouble meant slavery and oppression. Both were often the case for the Israelites.

If you study the history of the Israelites, there were times when their oppression by foreign nations lasted for *hundreds of years*. One would think that after just a few days of hardcore slavery the people would have thought to themselves, "That was stupid. We need God. Lack of intimacy with God is our true problem. We've been Complacent, Frustrated, Independent, and Rebellious for far too long. Why don't we try a different approach and return to the faithful place where we once found refuge and abundance?"

But, often times, they didn't choose to cut their cycle short. And we don't either. Usually we find something or someone else to blame for our current life circumstances. It's God's fault. Our boss's fault. Our spouse's fault. It's the current economy or our national leadership's responsibility.

We say things like "If only this wouldn't have happened" or "If they'd just do what they're supposed to do" or "I'll change *this* when *that* happens." There's always a scapegoat for the Trouble we've created and the blessings we feel like we deserve but aren't receiving.

My Own Rebellious Trouble

I've experienced more Trouble in life because of the spin cycle of Complacency, Frustration, Independence, and Rebellion than everyone reading this book could count on all their fingers and toes, combined. I've been suspended from school, had my license revoked, lost jobs, relationships, places to live, been arrested several times, gotten myself into serious debt, landed myself in the hospital on more than one occasion, lost the respect of my friends and peers, and allowed myself to be enslaved to many addictive, destructive behaviors.

Trouble comes in many shapes, sizes and forms. But they aren't always as blatant as those I've just listed. Sometimes Trouble can be very subtle. Nonetheless, self-inflicted Trouble and the spinning cycle of Complacency, Frustration, Independence, and Rebellion keeps us from experiencing God's best and from living in His *Sweet Spot*.

As I write this, God has blessed me in such a way that I don't have to work for the next couple of months while I spend dedicated time writing this book. My bills are payed; I just have to do a little side-work to pay for gas and groceries.

However, my budget for groceries has been relegated to eating dried, boxed pasta, along with whatever protein is least expensive to mix into the, otherwise, unflavored pasta. I eat the same thing, every day, for days on end. Why? Because I'm not putting the proper amount of time into the kind of work that pays enough to have a decent budget for healthy groceries.

My reasoning is because I'm trying to get this book written. That's why I don't have time to go make more Postmates, UberEATS, or DoorDash deliveries. That's why I don't have gas, grocery, or extra money to set aside for bills. But, in reality, there are days when I write very little.

In fact, just yesterday I neglected my morning devotional time and never logged into my Bible app. As such, my 131 day streak of reading a short devotional on this particular app was wiped out. My app says I now have a one-day reading streak. I got lots of writing done yesterday; but, I did it in my own, Independent (rather than dependent on God) way.

Not spending time in God's word is Complacency. Writing without that devoted time is Independence. I'm Frustrated over my finances when I'm not putting forth the effort to make the money I need to purchase healthy food. And, I blame it all on God by saying I don't have time because I'm writing His book.

Can you see where Trouble could be lurking?

In reality, however, I know God has called me to write this book. He has provided me some paid time off to get it done, and I'm really not hurting for anything—all things considered. I'm actually living in *God's Sweet Spot*, except for my lack of intimate time with Him yesterday.

I call it Complacency. The key is that I recognize my lack of intimate time with God and cut my cycle short. I don't have to continue down the slippery slope of that rut-ingrained spin cycle. I don't have to get Frustrated, become Independent, Rebellious, or experience self-inflicted Trouble. I just have to cut my cycle short and do what I did today, spend dedicated time with God.

What Kind of Trouble Are You In?

What kind of Trouble do you find yourself experiencing right now? Is it the kind of distress that occurs over and over again? Maybe the reason you chose to read this book was because this is the first time you ever truly considered your life may be in a spin cycle. Perhaps you were just looking for hope in the empty, howling wasteland that you've called life for way too long. Or, maybe you've never taken enough time to consider the reason you keep ending up in the same place.

Consider this verse:

> "Be sober [well balanced and self-disciplined], be alert and cautious at all times. That enemy of yours, the devil, prowls around like a roaring lion [fiercely hungry], seeking someone to devour" (1 Peter 5:8, AMP).

Any questions? If you want answers, keep reading. God has a special plan for your life and He is willing to move heaven and earth to see you become all He has planned for you. The first thing you need to do is take a self-analysis of where you are and learn to cut your cycle short.

The next couple of chapters will prepare you for the healing God has in store for your life. Then the second half of this book will walk you, step-by-step, into the greatest place you could ever imagine: *God's Sweet Spot*.

Selah (Pause for Reflection)

Take *15 Minutes* and Make this Chapter *Personal*

> *NOTE: Always keep a Bible, notebook, and pen ready.*
> ***Why?*** *I believe God will open himself up to you during this time of reflection, just as He does for me.*

How long have you been in a place of Rebellion, blaming everyone and everything for your life circumstances, but not taking the personal responsibility it takes to make a positive change?

- Take a moment to make a list of all the current "Trouble" you find yourself or your family in;

- Next to each troublesome way, make a note concerning who or what you've been blaming for your Troubles;

- Pray over each thing, asking God to show you specific ways you need to make changes in order to see His best for your life become a reality;

- Then, don't worry about eloquence. Find your own words to pray these powerful words of Scripture as a confession and commitment to God:

"Submit yourselves, then, to God. Resist the devil, and he will flee from you. Come near to God and he will come near to you. Wash your hands, you sinners, and purify your hearts, you double-minded. Grieve, mourn and wail. Change your laughter to mourning and your joy to gloom. Humble yourselves before the Lord, and he will lift you up" (James 4:7-10, NLT).

Chapter Eleven

I GIVE UP!

"The greatness of a man's power is the measure of his surrender."
~ William Boothe, Founder of the Salvation Army[14]

Do you know the universal sign of surrender? It's been in every gangster movie you've ever seen. When either the police or a criminal catch somebody by surprise, what's the next move?

Unless you're a Marvel character, Jason Statham, Liam Neeson, Jet Lee, Sarah Connor, Dirty Harry, Wonder Woman, James Bond (I like Sean Connery the best), Rambo, Indiana Jones, or some other hero-type, what do you do? YOU PUT YOUR HANDS UP!

I've seen different versions of the hands-in-the-air surrender. Sometimes the hands are straight up in the air. Most of the time, however, we see elbows bent with hands in the air in a formation that looks like a goalpost on a football field.

It's Harder Than It Looks

Let's try an experiment. Put both hands in the air, with your elbows bent like you're making a goalpost on a football field. Now hold your hands in that Surrendered position for as long as you can, counting the seconds as you go. Seriously! I want you to know how long you can handle a position of Surrender.

I tried it. I set my phone's stopwatch to see how long I could go. It took 3 minutes, 24 seconds before my shoulders started to ache. By 4 minutes, 25 seconds my arms were starting to sag. At the 8 minute, 55 second mark, I was ready to drop my arms and let my assailant shoot me!

I'm sure that if this weren't just an experiment and my adrenaline was pumping, I could have gone another few minutes. But, as I type this, my arms are still aching.

In the same way, our Surrender to God is often short lived. We make promises, pray with sincerity of heart, and our own strength still fails us. *Surrender to God is our choice, but we can't do it in our own strength.*

I've been in some pretty low places in my life. I've lost many things, including my health, my positive Christian witness, and many cherished relationships. Because of the Trouble my Rebellion brought, I've prayed hundreds of prayers of Surrender.

I remember praying all day about particular areas of weakness and promising God that *today* would be the day I'd give in to His best for my life. I still failed that day.

Sure, I asked for God's help, His healing, His deliverance. But, each day, I'd take things into my own hands and find myself deeper and deeper in a rut of self-destruction.

How Long Does It Take?

There's a story in the Bible about a wonderful man of God. He'd made plenty of mistakes in life and paid the price for His Independence and Rebellion. At the time our story picks up, this man had, however, become a pinnacle of God's power. He was Surrendered to God's will and purpose for his life.

After hundreds of years of Rebellion and the Trouble that slavery and oppression brings, God's people cried out for help. They were ready to Surrender. So God used a man named Moses to lead them out of captivity. Instead of the bondage of Egyptian rule, the destination God had in store for His people was a place of abundance, freedom, and serenity. A destination the Bible describes as "flowing with milk and honey," where a single cluster of grapes had to be attached to a pole and took two men to carry the great abundance God was graciously giving them (see Numbers 13:23-27).

Though the Israelite people were excited about the abundance of wealth and harvest God had promised would be theirs, they were also afraid of the size of the people who could eat such clusters of grapes. What if they tried to take the land and were overtaken by the monstrosity of people who lived there?

As such, the people of God took the route of Independence and Rebellion—once again—and decided to turn away from the promises and blessings of God. This meant more Trouble. Now, they'd have to war against invading nations for forty years before they would Surrender to God once again.

That's a long time to keep your hands in your pockets, instead of placing them in the air! But Moses was different. Though the people had Rebelled, he kept his hands in the air. One story, in particular, is fascinating to me:

> "While the people of Israel were still at Rephidim, the warriors of Amalek attacked them. Moses commanded Joshua, 'Choose some men to go out and fight the army of Amalek for us. Tomorrow, I will stand at the top of the hill, holding the staff of God in my hand. So Joshua did what Moses had commanded and fought the army of Amalek. Meanwhile, Moses, Aaron, and Hur climbed to the top of a nearby hill. *As long as Moses held up the staff in his hand, the Israelites had the advantage. But whenever he dropped his hand, the Amalekites gained the advantage.* Moses' arms soon became so tired he could no longer hold them up. So Aaron and Hur found a stone for him to sit on. *Then they stood on each side of Moses, holding up his hands.* So his hands held steady until sunset. As a result, Joshua overwhelmed the army of Amalek in battle" (Exodus 17:8-13, NLT, *emphases mine*).

Moses was Surrendered to God's will. He knew what he had to do. And he knew his Surrender didn't have a time limit. He simply had to have a heart that was positioned for willingness. BUT, he also knew he couldn't do it alone.

How, Then, Do We Do It?

We all need help when it comes to surrendering our own selfish, self-centered, me-me-me, attitudes and actions. In our own strength it is impossible to keep a posture of "hands in the air" Surrender.

In many cases, we may need the help of others—whether counselors, truly grounded Christian friends, pastors, or even medical help. All of these are helpful. Each, however, will also prove to be impotent without the power of God working in our lives.

God saved the Israelite on that fateful day, but it took a lot of faith, help from others, and the hearts of at least three Surrendered men to see God's purpose and blessings unfold. As you consider the help you may need, also consider the empowerment that awaits you when you fully Surrender to God and begin following His defined ways:

> "Submit yourselves, then, to God. Resist the devil, and
> he will flee from you" (James 4:7, NIV).

The phrase "submit yourselves" is translated from the Greek word "hupotasso," which is an *active verb* meaning to submit oneself to another's control, *continuously*. Just to make to the point clear, an active verb is not the same thing as a regular verb. I can chew a piece of gum. In this case "chew" is the verb. At some point, however, that gum is going to lose its flavor and I'm going to spit it out. When it comes to most gum, the verb *chew* is something I do once, because unless the gum was made by an Oompa Loompa, continuously chewing simply wouldn't make sense. An active verb is different. It is something we do on an ongoing basis, not something we do once and stop. As such, "submit yourselves" means we are to give God control in every moment of every day.

The crazy thing is that God asks for our continued submission to Him, but also says that we have a responsibility too. First, we give up all control to God; then, we do what He says: we resist the temptation. As a result, the overwhelming result is victory as we see the Complacency, Independence, Rebellion, and Trouble dissipate because we know we don't have to worry about being in control. That's God's role. Our role is to Surrender to Him with complete obedience.

We could end the story here by giving up control and acting in obedience. But, sometimes it just doesn't seem that easy; so, we lower our hands. This is where we have to *resist the devil* and be persistent.

> "So humble yourselves under the mighty power of God, and at the right time he will lift you up in honor" (1 Peter 5:6, NLT).

As before, "humble yourselves" is an active verb. Humbling ourselves in the moment is not so difficult. What we have a hard time with is God's timing. As such, we often give up after a while. Instead, the answer to our problems will only be found when we keep praying, keep submitting, keep humbling ourselves, keep seeking God, and keep being obedient. Then, at just the right moment, God will bring all things together for our good.

Complete surrender is not easy. It's easy to say the words, mumble a prayer, and still stay on our own personal course of destruction. BUT, I want to encourage you. True Surrender is the only step that will lead you to *God's Sweet Spot*. The key is remembering you can't truly Surrender without a continuously submitted heart and a complete reliance on God to help you follow through.

In the next two chapters, we'll see how God responds to a Surrendered heart and review how we got to the cavernous rut we're currently in. Never forget, *you need to know where you've been to determine where you never want to go again.*

Afterwards, get ready for the adventure of a lifetime. We're going to dive into the deep end of *God's Sweet Spot* and—with His help—we're going to learn how to swim (maybe even walk on water).

Selah (Pause for Reflection)

Take *15 Minutes* and Make this Chapter *Personal*

> *NOTE: Always keep a Bible, notebook, and pen ready.* **Why?** *I believe God will open himself up to you during this time of reflection, just as He does for me.*

Getting to know God leads to Trusting Him. Trusting Him leads to an intimacy of love that cannot be explained in human terms. That's why there are so many Biblical passages in the chronicles of this writing.

I want to teach you to know God. If you haven't already, you may want to go back and find every Scripture quoted, make a note of the Biblical reference, and start writing these verses down on note cards. I have a whole stack of them, written on the front and the back. They keep me steady, focused, and grounded in true Trust.

Here are two more passages worth reading and worth praying over your own life and circumstances. Remember, God knows your heart. Fill it with His Words and you will discover *God's Sweet Spot*:

> "Have mercy on me, O God, because of your unfailing love. Because of your great compassion, blot out the stain of my sins. Wash me clean from my guilt. Purify me from my sin. For I recognize my rebellion; it haunts me day and night. Against you, and you alone, have I sinned; I have done what is evil in your sight. You will be proved right in what you say, and your judgment against me is just... Purify me from my sins, and I will be clean; wash me, and I will be whiter than snow. Oh, give me back my joy again; you have broken me—now let me rejoice. Don't keep looking at my sins. Remove the stain

of my guilt. Create in me a clean heart, O God. Renew a loyal spirit within me" (Psalm 51:1-4, 7-10, NLT)

"You made me; you created me. Now give me the sense to follow your command" (Psalm 119:73, NLT).

Chapter Twelve

HERE "I AM" TO SAVE THE DAY

*"Mr. Trouble never hangs around, when he hears this
Mighty sound, 'HERE I COME TO SAVE THE DAY!'
That means that Mighty Mouse is on the way!"*
~ Mighty Mouse Theme Song[15]

I'm sure there has to be at least *one* odd child out there, but what kid doesn't like watching cartoons? Back in the day, it was Bugs Bunny, Wile E. Coyote, Elmer Fudd, Pepé Le Pew, the Tasmanian Devil, Yosemite Sam, Porky Pig, Grape Ape, George of the Jungle, and, yes, Mighty Mouse. Most cartoon characters had some kind of flaw or odd characteristic, like Daffy Duck's lisp and nonsensical ways. But Mighty Mouse was different. When there was trouble, you'd always hear those famous words, "Here I come to save the day!"

As a play on his declaration, I decided to entitle this chapter, "Here I AM to Save the Day." Though our Rescue is dependent on our genuine, continual Surrender and our personal commitment to do whatever it takes, the only One who can Rescue us is God. Whether it's anger, depression, financial stress, health issues, pride, selfishness, unruly kids, a disrespectful spouse, an addiction, or whatever name you want to put on your struggle, the God of the Bible, referred to as the Great "I AM," is our ultimate refuge, redeemer, and Rescue.

God knows our dispositions, and He loves us anyway. God knew His people would turn from Him time and time again, but I love this promise He made to His people (including you and me):

> "Therefore, say to the people of Israel: 'I am the Lord. I will free you from your oppression and will *rescue* you from your slavery in Egypt. I will redeem you with a powerful arm and great acts of judgment'" (Exodus 6:6, NLT, *emphasis mine*).

God followed through on His promise. After the Israelites had Rebelled—time and time again—God brought them to the place where treachery, defeat, and Trouble could be put behind them. Though they were responsible for their own demise, He came through on His Word and allowed them to enter into the "land of milk and honey." A place of freedom, of abundance, prosperity, and—ultimately—His *Sweet Spot*!

The only thing that stood in the Israelites' way was the Jordan River—and it was at complete flood-stage. Millions of people needed to pass through these waters to finally inherit God's promise, but the rising tide seemed impossible to pass.

So what did God do? He miraculously parted the waters. In a similar way God had parted the Red Sea (Sea of Reeds) for Moses as the Israelites exited their oppression and slavery in Egypt, God opened the waters for Moses' successor, Joshua. The waters divided, and the riverbed dried up in order to allow nearly two and a half million of God's people to finally enter into their promised land.

The people had come to a place of Surrender. And God came through—just as He'd promised!

What Being Rescued Looks Like

Not all Rescuing looks the same. Sometimes, the relief from our Troubles is immediate. Other times, there seems to be a lapse in God's heroic action. As you consider God's timing, one thing to keep in mind is that God doesn't always Rescue us from the consequences of our actions. However, just because everything doesn't become perfect for us in an instant doesn't mean our Rescuer isn't actively working things for our good (see Romans 8:28). Additionally, we need to be aware of the level of our Surrender. Does our Surrender resemble handsfully in the air or drooping arms? Are we continuously making conscious decisions to move away from the way we've always done things and toward complete, submitted obedience?

There are times, however, when we don't know what God wants us to do in particular uncertain circumstances. In these instances, it can be difficult to be completely submitted to God's plan for our lives when we don't know what that plan is. In this case, if you don't know what God wants you to do in your specific moment of desperation, pray and wait.

Waiting can be hard. Yet some form of the word "wait" appears up to 160 times in the King James Version of the Bible. That seems to be a lot. Fortunately, many instances of the word *wait* in the Bible means to "wait with hopeful expectation."

I've discovered the more something is repeated in the Bible, the more important it is. And, as I've reasoned reiterated themes in the Bible over the years, I believe certain themes reoccur more often than others because God knows these things will be difficult for us to do; so, He encourages us with repetition. As such, sometimes God answers in an instant. Other times, our Rescue depends upon our *waiting with hopeful expectation*.

I remember a time when I threw my hands up in complete Surrender to God concerning some very overt sexual sin in my life. I confessed my sin and asked for God's help. Immediately, God took those desires away from me. I chose to get off all the dating sites I was on, stopped making booty calls to the women I knew I could always fall back on, and—this may sound a little graphic—I even refrained from self-gratification. In this case the Rescue was IMMEDIATE.

I also recall when I had gotten myself into $40,000 worth of consumer debt—living *way* beyond my means. Again, I threw my hands up in Surrender. I asked God for greater provision and for Him to alleviate my desire for *keeping up with the Jones'*.

To my dismay, instead of seeing an increase in my income, I saw a dramatic decline. I knew, however, that I was Surrendered to God's will in the area of my finances and that He would come through.

I still used my credit cards for emergencies, but determined to stop making impulse purchases. It took years to pay that $40,000 debt down to $20,000 before God intervened and took care of the rest.

Some might say that the actual intervention and Rescue came when I was able to—through an insurance settlement—pay off the remaining $20,000. And, in some ways I agree. I also believe God's might was shown during the years when I Surrendered my purchasing impulses and He allowed me to pay off the first half of my debt by living on less than I previously thought I deserved.

What is it that Troubles you? Assign a name to it. Name the sin. Name the Troublesome circumstance. Then, Surrender yourself and your circumstances to God and commit to doing things His way. If you do, the great "I AM" *will* save the day.

A MONUMENTAL Event

At times, we can fall into the mindful trap of believing we've conquered our own Troublesome circumstances, attitudes, or actions (see Deuteronomy 8:17-18). When this is the case, we're probably still in a state of Independence or have reverted to that point in our cycle. The Bible, however, reminds us that *all good things come from God* (see James 1:17). As such, our attitude should not be one of Independence, but one of gratefulness.

The people of Israel realized the source of their Rescue and constructed a monument that would gratefully remind them of God's saving power:

> When all the people had crossed the Jordan, the Lord said to Joshua, 'Now choose twelve men, one from each tribe. Tell them, "Take twelve stones from the very place where the priests are standing in the middle of the Jordan. Carry them out and pile them up at the place where you will camp tonight."'... So the men did as Joshua had commanded them. They took twelve stones from the middle of the Jordan River, one for each tribe, just as the Lord had told Joshua. They carried them to the place where they camped for the night and *constructed the memorial there*" (Joshua 4:1-3, 8, NLT, *emphasis mine*).

I would emphatically suggest that you determine to set up a *monument* of remembrance and gratitude each time you recognize God's intervention in the midst of your Troubled times. This act of memorializing God's grace and goodness will act as a reminder to you the next time you're in Trouble, in need, or have slipped back into the vicious spin cycle that leads you away from *God's Sweet Spot*.

I'm not suggesting you make a pile of twelve rocks each time God comes to your Rescue, but the act of celebrating God's handiwork is vital to sustaining a life characterized by fulfillment, peace and Trust. Your monument may look different from mine, but here are a few suggestions to get you thinking:

- Find a large, clear, decorative vase and determine a place of honor for it in your home. Then, each time God Rescues you or intervenes on your behalf—whether the Trouble be of your own doing or circumstantial—place a rock in the vase. The rock may be rough, depicting the intensity of the Trouble from which God Rescued you. Or, it may be a smooth river stone or one like you'd purchase at a craft store or gem mine. In this case the representation might be of how God smoothed things out for you when you needed Him most;

- Purchase a nice composition book or journal. Take some time picking it out because this is a memorial you are building to God and His powerful workings in your life. A special place of storage or display should also be considered. Then, each time God comes to the Rescue—again in answer to self-inflicted Trouble or life circumstances—journal about the experience. Date each entry and describe the circumstances behind your Trouble, your act of Surrender, and how God came to the Rescue;

- A treasure chest is also a great way to build a monument to God's grace and goodness. Again, whether your Troubled time is because of your own Rebellion or an answer to prayer during a tough time in your life, find a piece of memorabilia that will remind you of how God came to the Rescue. Perhaps He delivered you from an addiction to pornography. In this case, you may put a white ribbon in your treasure chest to remind you of sexual purity. Maybe your Trouble stemmed from a self-centered attitude. A small compass may work as a reminder that you've been misguided in your ways. A magnifying glass may remind you of when God opened your eyes to a particular area you needed to Surrender to Him. The possibilities are endless.

These are just a few suggestions. Feel free to come up with your own way of building a monument of gratitude and remembrance. Maybe you'll actually decide to find a place in your yard where you place a large stone each time God comes to the Rescue. Whatever your choice, the key is to memorialize God's mercy and faithfulness, so you always have a reminder that when you live your life Surrendered to God, the great "I AM" always comes to the Rescue.

Selah (Pause for Reflection)

Take *15 Minutes* and Make this Chapter *Personal*

> *NOTE: Always keep a Bible, notebook, and pen ready.* ***Why?*** *I believe God will open himself up to you during this time of reflection, just as He does for me.*

Though you may often be your own worst enemy, there are evil powers at work that want to tear you down. The devil knows your Achilles heel and will exploit it every chance he gets.

As you consciously and continuously submit your will to God's best plans for your life and sincerely Surrender yourself to Him, the following prayer is one you should write down, carry with you wherever you go, and pray daily for the rest of your life:

> "I am praying to you because I know you will answer, O God. Bend down and listen *as I pray*. Show me your unfailing love in wonderful ways. By your mighty power you ***rescue*** those who seek refuge from their enemies. Guard me as you would guard your own eyes. Hide me in the shadow of your wings" (Psalm 17:6-8, NLT, ***emphasis mine***).

Chapter Thirteen

HOME SWEET HOME

*"There's no place like home. There's no place like home.
There's no place like home."*
~ Dorothy, from The Wizard of Oz[16]

Recently, I took a trip to the Cleveland area of Ohio to visit some friends. Though I grew up in North Carolina and currently reside there now, I lived in the Cleveland area for several years. It was there that I made some of the best friends I've ever known.

The trip was an eight-hour drive, but it was worth it because I was able to reconnect with friends I haven't seen in years. My stay was for just over a week. During that time, I went to the church I was a part of when I lived there. I also had lunch with friends, had dinner with friends, watched football with friends, made some new friends, and slept in a small bed at my best friend's house that was so much more comfortable than the larger one I sleep in at home.

I had such a great time that I really didn't want to leave. If I could take my daughter with me and—somehow—lessen the snow accumulation during the winters by half, I'd move back in a heartbeat.

When it was finally time for me to make the eight-hour drive back, I dreaded it. I really don't like driving. When I do, however, I don't stop. I just want to get to my destination without delay.

After a grueling drive and ending up with a very numb derriere, I finally reached my destination. I was home again. And, as Dorothy, in the movie *The Wizard of Oz* says, "There's no place like home."

Similar to Dorothy's iconic declaration, there's also an old saying, "Home is where the heart is." Where is your heart today? Though you may have a physical address—and really like it there—the best place to keep your heart and home is in *God's Sweet Spot*.

> "Bless the Lord, O my soul, and all that is within me, bless his holy name! Bless the Lord, O my soul, and forget not all his benefits, who forgives all your iniquity, who heals all your diseases, *who redeems your life from the pit...*" (Psalm 103:1-4a, ESV, *emphasis mine*).

In this passage we hear the voice of someone who calls *God's Sweet Spot* home. It's also the voice of a man who had committed adultery, murder, shown unmerited favoritism with his children, and the list goes on. But the author of the words, King David, also knew what it meant to be in full Surrender to God and to be Rescued. He knew what it meant to be Rescued from his enemies, from his own deceitful heart, and from what he calls the "pit."

When you've been Rescued from the pit, you know what it means to fully Trust in God again. To be in His *Sweet Spot*, again. But, sometimes, the pit we find ourselves in isn't of our own doing. When we find ourselves in this kind of dismay—in the kind of Trouble that comes at us from nowhere—staying in a place of complete Trust in God can be difficult.

Blindsided

The Psalmist mentions one such blindsiding and Troublesome pit when he refers to diseases. And, yes; God does heal all of our diseases. For some that healing is miraculously immediate. For others, God uses doctors, medications, and various procedures to bring about healing. There are also many whose diseases may not be healed until they get to heaven. Even so, healing *will* come!

Whatever God's perfect choice of timing for healing the diseases in or around you, a heart that is fully Surrendered to God will always find ways to be a blessing to others—even when riddled with physical disease. The key is Trusting God, no matter our circumstances. I know, because I've seen it. I've seen both ends of the spectrum. I've known people with chronic ailments who always complained. They made sure to pass some of their misery along to anyone who'd listen. I've also known sweet spirited people who didn't know if their disease would allow them another year, month, week, or day to live; yet, they used their limited time to reflect God's love as they fully Trusted God with each second they had left.

> "...the righteous has hope and confidence and a refuge [with God] even in death" (Proverbs 14:32, AMP).

It may be hard to fully Trust God during times of Trouble that blindside us, whether enduring ailing diseases or some other unexpected distress. These are times when we need to return to the *monument* we built. The one that reminds us of God's grace, His goodness, His faithfulness, and His love. Where is that vase full of rocks? That journal's accountings? That treasure box of mementoes, reminding you of all the ways that God has come through for you in the past?

> "Remember [with gratitude] His marvelous deeds which
> He has done..." (1 Chronicles 16:12a, AMP).

Homecoming

When you have come full circle, through whatever spin cycle or life circumstances you find yourself in, the best place to go is home. Home to a place of Trusting again and living in God's best. If the rut or pit you've been living in is because you've allowed yourself to stray away from God's absolute best plan for your life, an even better route than *coming full circle* is to simply *cut your cycle short* and go home. Return to *God's Sweet Spot*.

Take a moment to still your heart and mind. Get away from all distractions and read these verses aloud, realizing that these words are being spoken to you by God Himself:

> "I love all who love me. Those who search will surely
> find me... My gifts are better than gold, even the purest
> gold, my wages better than sterling silver!" (Proverbs
> 8:17, 19, NLT)

Trust is a verb and a place of habitation, but it's also a state of mind. When you are fully Surrendered and have seen God move in your life—even Rescue you from the pit—the place you'll find yourself in is better than any amount of gold or silver the world could ever afford you. The *secret place* of God is a real place. It's a dwelling place you can make your home. Your permanent home. Even if you wander away, momentarily, you can always make the journey home.

Staying at Home

Learning how to cut your spin cycle short is the key to returning to a place of Surrender and Trust. But, sometimes we wander away. We get Complacent, Frustrated, Independent, Rebellious, and in Trouble. The wandering usually begins with Complacency. Don't let yourself get there. Just as God warned the Israelites, He is warning you and me:

> "When you have eaten your fill, be sure to praise the Lord your God for the good land he has given you. But that is the time to be careful! Beware that in your plenty you do not forget the Lord your God and disobey his commands, regulations, and decrees that I am giving you today. For when you have become full and prosperous and have built fine homes to live in, and when your flocks and herds have become very large and your silver and gold have multiplied along with everything else, be careful! Do not become proud at that time and forget the Lord your God, who rescued you from slavery in the land of Egypt" (Deuteronomy 8:10-14, NLT).

The best advice I can give you—and that God is giving us in this passage—is to STAY AT HOME or, at least, learn to cut your cycle short. The rest of this book is dedicated to the journey God inspired me to share. We'll learn, step-by-step, how to get into *God's Sweet Spot,* how to stay there on a day-to-day basis, learn to realize when we're getting off course, get back *home* as quickly as possible, and discover how to move *from the frustration of running-on-empty to the fulfillment of life overflowing.*

Selah (Pause for Reflection)

Take *15 Minutes* and Make this Chapter *Personal*

> *NOTE: Always keep a Bible, notebook, and pen ready.*
> ***Why?*** *I believe God will open himself up to you during this time of reflection, just as He does for me.*

A while back I found myself back on the hamster wheel. I was back in the washing machine and on the spin cycle.

The rut I found myself in was a familiar one. One that I tried to ignore or just hoped would go away. But it didn't.

It all started with Complacency in my relationship with God. But I jumped straight from Complacency to Rebellion and Trouble. I felt bone-dry empty. Empty within my soul. I don't like that place. I never want to go there again. That's why I'm writing this book. I want to help you—and me—learn how to stay at *home* or, at least, not wander too far off before we return.

God is gracious and He is faithful. When I finally threw my hands up in Surrender, He Rescued and delivered me once again.

As I fully Surrendered to Him, I felt a sense of peace come over me like I've never felt. I felt as though God was telling me that I was entering into a season of great favor in His sight. I began speaking words of life (see Proverbs 18:21) over my current circumstances. These are the words I am proclaiming as Truth and I'd encourage you to pray these words, aloud, every day, until you see the fruit of your words become a reality in your own life:

> "Father God, I love You and I know You love me. I know You have incredible things in store for me as I continue to Surrender to You. As such, I speak Your redemption, restoration, wisdom, prosperity, favor, and good health over my life. In Jesus' name, I claim the fruit of my words as Your Truth and promise, because I Trust in You. Amen."

I have this prayer—written on a notecard—on the dash of my car. I stuck it in the little slot between the dash and the instrument panel. It's on the side of the tachometer (RPMs), not the side where it shows my gas level and speed limit (I need to know how much gas I have and how fast I'm going).

Every day, when I get in the car, I pray the above prayer over my life. Perhaps you will benefit from doing so too.

Chapter Fourteen

DRASTIC MEASURES, BABY STEPS

"If we desire to avoid insult, we must be able to repel it; if we desire to secure peace, one of the most powerful instruments of our rising prosperity, it must be known, that we are at all times ready for War."
~ *George Washington*[17]

I love to watch a good movie. I'm not very fond of movies that are completely subtitled, horror movies, and I believe many indie films should stay just that: independent (with a few exceptions). However, I do like most other genres. I enjoy comedy, suspense, drama, romance, thrillers, westerns, action, and even many of the newer animated movies.

Sometimes we group several genres together and lump them into a particular category. One such category is what we often refer to as "chick flicks." Though I've never heard the term "guy flicks," certain genres—like action films—definitely fall into that category.

One movie that's *not* an action flick, but definitely falls into the guy category, is the movie *What About Bob?*[18] (at least for guys of my generation). The movie's primary characters are a Bob Wiley, played by Bill Murray, and Dr. Leo Marvin, a psychiatrist played by Richard Dreyfuss.

During an initial assessment of Bob, Dr. Marvin diagnoses Bob as "an almost paralyzed, multiphobic personality that is in a constant state of panic." Dr. Marvin goes on to recommend a book he's recently written to help Bob through his multiple crises. The book is called, "Baby Steps." Dr. Marvin explains the premise of the book by saying, "It means setting small, reasonable goals for yourself. One day at a time. One tiny step at a time."

That's what we're going to do for the remainder of our journey together. We're going to take *baby steps* toward a place of Surrender and Trust. Toward finding peace in the midst of a Troubled world. Jesus said, "I have told you these things, so that in me you may have peace. *In this world you will have trouble.* But take heart! I have overcome the world" (John 16:33, NIV, *emphasis mine*).

We will have Troubles in this life. Some Troubles we have created for ourselves, but others exist because we live in a Troubled world. Jesus tells us, however, that we can have peace in the midst of our Troubles. We just have to look to Him for the answers, the Rescue, and the help we need along the way. He tells us in this verse that the war has already been won. We still have battles to fight, but our Trust can be found in the fact that, when all is said and done, Jesus and those who choose to believe in, trust in, cling to, and rely on Him already have true victory over the War.

What Steps Are You Taking?

For some, the baby steps we'll be taking will be arduous. We are not use to relying on anyone but ourselves, draining others along the way. Those who fall into this category are not use to depending on God. We believe in Him, but our actions—and inactions—often deny what we say we believe.

Ponder these questions:

- How do you become a solution to your own problem?
- If you know that *you* are your own problem, how do you fix your own problem?

The answer is a double-edged sword. Only God can heal you of whatever your affliction may be. But, as I've stated before, you must participate.

I'm guessing there are a few readers who are simply looking for a bandage. A quick fix. If you'd known you could just skip to the *baby steps* section of this book, you'd have bypassed the lessons on *why* you keep ending up in the same old place. Perhaps you are in a hurry to simply find the answer, but haven't considered the impact of the short times of reflection at the end of each chapter. Maybe you haven't taken the time to pray the prayers, read the Scriptures, and definitely felt awkward saying things aloud, like "*I have hopeful expectation for my life because I have restful confidence in God's plan for my future.*"

I have a friend who used to always say, "*Let me know how that works out for you.*" I never heard a tenor of sarcasm in his voice when he said it; but, when he spoke those words, you always knew his implications were that you were acting Independently and that you might want to reconsider your next move.

The Bible puts it this way:

> "We are destroying sophisticated arguments and every exalted and proud thing that sets itself up against the [true] knowledge of God, and we are taking every thought and purpose captive to the obedience of Christ" (2 Corinthians 10:5, AMP).

If you're truly looking for a life-change and want to stop feeling the Frustration of running-on-empty, you may want to consider slowing down a bit. Reconsider your thoughts and the way you've always done things. Then, Surrender your thought-life to God. Perhaps you would benefit from rereading the preceding chapters, truly considering your own patterns, and take the time to react to the "Selah-Vie" (life reflections) at the end of each chapter.

I want you to succeed. More than that, God wants you to come to Him in full Surrender and discover His best for your life. Only then will you find true healing rather than a piece of gauze and some medical tape.

The Apostle Paul uses these words to put God's ultimate plans for you to succeed in perspective:

> "I pray that your love will overflow more and more, and that you will *keep on growing* in knowledge and understanding. *For I want you to understand what really matters...*" (Philippians 1:9-10a, NLT, *emphases mine*).

What really matters is *growing*. Not whatever is on your plate today. If you desire true life change, seek it with all of your heart, *learn what really matters*, and *Trust God to do His part*. It's your choice. You can either allow this journey be arduous because you want a quick fix and because of your Independent nature or you can choose to throw your hands up in Surrender and take the necessary steps.

Besides those who want a quick fix and may struggle in moving forward if they continue doing things their own way, there are also two other categories of readers. There are those of us who—though we may struggle with our Independent nature at first—will embrace the baby steps, choosing the freedom of Trusting God instead of our Independent ways. As we do so, we will begin to see a brighter future ahead of us.

Recognition will also be birthed in us that enlightens us to the fact that we are *already* living in *God's Sweet Spot* as we diligently pursue Him with every baby step we take.

Then there's another category of readers who will take every inspired word to heart and *run* with diligence. We are so sick and tired of being sick and tired that we're ready to do whatever it takes to finally land (and stay) in a place where fulfilment and life overflowing become a reality.

Consider the following three verses and determine which best describes where you are right now:

- "Test and evaluate yourselves to see whether you are in the faith and living your lives as [*committed*] believers. Examine yourselves [not me]! Or do you not recognize this about yourselves [by an ongoing experience] that Jesus Christ is in you— *unless indeed you fail the test* and are rejected as counterfeit?" (2 Corinthians 13:5, AMP, *emphases mine*).

- "For this very reason, make every effort to add to your faith goodness; and to goodness, knowledge; and to knowledge, self-control; and to self-control, perseverance; and to perseverance, godliness; and to godliness, mutual affection; and to mutual affection, love. For if you possess these qualities in increasing measure, *they will keep you from being ineffective and unproductive* in your knowledge of our Lord Jesus Christ" (2 Peter 1:5-8, NIV, *emphasis mine*)

- "Don't you realize that in a race everyone runs, but only one person gets the prize? So *run to win*! All athletes are disciplined in their training. They do it to win a prize that will fade away, but we do it for an eternal prize. So *I run with purpose in every step*..." (1 Corinthians 9:24-26a, NLT, *emphases mine*).

The sooner you discover where you are and determine to fully Surrender to God, the sooner you'll land in *God's Sweet Spot* of hopeful expectation and complete Trust.

Drastic Measures

If you want to see a drastic change in your current—and future—life circumstances, it will take drastic measures. I don't know about you, but I want to live a better life than I've ever lived. Sure there will be hardship along the way. There will be disappointments. But facing those trials with a genuine Trust in God's love, grace, and faithfulness—believing He will always be there for us—is where "peace that surpasses all understanding" (see Philippians 4:7) begins.

Like it or not, the steps you choose to take from this day forward will determine whether you continue to live in desperation, fear, or so focused on yourself that you never realize God's best for you, or whether you find true contentment in life. You can choose to take on the conflict—with God as your lead—or you can be overtaken by the enemy of your soul. Either way, a battle is already being waged.

❖ **Internal Conflict**

Often the battle is within:

> "Temptation comes *from our own desires*, which entice us and drag us away. These desires give birth to sinful actions. And when sin is allowed to grow, it gives birth to death" (James 1:14-15, NLT, *emphasis mine*).

When our own selfish, self-seeking ways lead us into Trouble, Jesus gives us strong warnings. He tells us that if our eye causes us to sin, we should gouge it out. Or, if our hand causes us to sin we should cut it off. He says that it is better to be without an eye or a hand than to be condemned to hell because of our own selfish desires (see Matthew 5:29-30). Of course, the emphasis of every word is not literal in these verses. Instead, the prominent point is if the battle we are facing comes from within, we must take whatever *drastic measures* necessary to alter our path.

On the other hand, Jesus' indication of condemnation to hell *is* meant to be literal for those who refuse to accept His forgiveness. But, even those of us who have chosen to receive God's gift of grace can still experience a life characterized by Frustration when we choose to do things our own way.

❖ External Combat

Though there are times when the battle waged against our own Complacent, Independent, Frustrated, and Rebellious selves is internal, there is also an external component that is *always* a part of the fight. This external component is a spiritual one.

> "For we are not wrestling with flesh and blood [contending only with physical opponents], but against the despotisms, against the powers, against [the master spirits who are] the world rulers of this present darkness, against the spirit forces of wickedness in the heavenly (supernatural) sphere" (Ephesians 6:12, AMPC).

The devil knows your weaknesses and he will prey on them. And it's not just the devil. He has a whole army of fallen angels who are under his command. They are evil "master spirits" who want to rob you of your joy, peace, contentment, and who will whisper lies into your ears. The devil will try to convince you that you'll never change, never get better, never accomplish anything, never get ahead, and never—ever—find true peace. But know this: Jesus declared the devil to be the "father of lies" (see John 8:42-44).

The Bible tells us that the only way to engage in battle with this evil lying demon and his wicked minions is to *equip ourselves*. Some versions use the terminology of putting on "the full armor of God" (see Ephesians 6:13-17, NIV). Much of what we'll be learning over the next several chapters will equip you to win every battle these wicked powers wage against you, including the Apostle Paul's addition of this directive to our battle plans:

> "...prayer is essential in this ongoing warfare. Pray hard and long. Pray for your brothers and sisters. Keep your eyes open. Keep each other's spirits up so that no one falls behind or drops out" (Ephesians 6:18, The Message).

As such our first baby step is going to be learning how to pray. How to pray effectual prayers. Prayers that matter. Prayers that are not self-seeking. Prayers that will change your life, forever.

Will you Surrender yourself, fully, to God and join me on this journey?

Selah (Pause for Reflection)

Take *15 Minutes* and Make this Chapter *Personal*

> *NOTE: Always keep a Bible, notebook, and pen ready.*
> ***Why?*** *I believe God will open himself up to you during this time of reflection, just as He does for me.*

To ready yourself for battle, I suggest reading the following passage, truly discerning how ready you currently are:

> "Be prepared. You're up against far more than you can handle on your own. Take all the help you can get, every weapon God has issued, so that when it's all over but the shouting you'll still be on your feet. Truth, righteousness, peace, faith, and salvation are more than words. Learn how to apply them. You'll need them throughout your life. God's Word is an indispensable weapon. In the same way, prayer is essential in this ongoing warfare. Pray hard and long. Pray for your brothers and sisters. Keep your eyes open. Keep each other's spirits up so that no one falls behind or drops out" (Ephesians 6:13-18, The Message).

Notice that the passage says that our weapons (or armor) for battle are not to be treated as mere words on a page. We must learn how to use them. They are indispensable.

As such, take a moment to pray and ask God to show you how ready you are *or* how much preparation you still need in order to fight the good fight and wrestle your way past the evil schemes the devil uses to keep you away from *God's Sweet Spot*.

Then, write God a short letter. It need not be more than a paragraph or two. Confess to Him the areas in which you know you are weak and ask Him to help you, because God is excited, ready, and waiting to help you find your way back *home*.

Chapter Fifteen

PRAY, PRAY, PRAY (AND THEN PRAY AGAIN)

> *"I have been driven many times upon my knees by the overwhelming conviction that I had no where else to go. My own wisdom and that of all about me seemed insufficient for that day."*
> ~ Abraham Lincoln[17]

I seem to be accident prone. I've broken my left leg, my left arm (twice), ribs, my nose, toes, and fingers. My last break was my first finger on my right hand, which is my dominant hand.

After over a week and a half of swollenness, stiffness, immobility, keeping my index finger iced and in a splint, I sought God's healing through prayer. I couldn't take it any longer. The inability to use my finger was hindering many of my regular activities—including writing. It was a Sunday afternoon when I prayed God would miraculously heal my finger by the next day. Can you guess what happened next?

Monday morning, I took the splint off and I was able to bend my finger over 50 percent of the way. Prior to my prayer, I couldn't get it to budge, even with force!

Perhaps you've experienced a miraculous answer to prayer. I've had many answers to prayer like this one, but far too many Christian believers haven't experienced the kind of answers to prayer that I've received. Or, perhaps they didn't recognize the answer. Instead, they chalked it up to coincidence or some other notion. Perhaps the biggest reason, however, that many people don't see answers to their prayers is simply because they don't pray with the kind of *hopeful expectation* that God will actually intervene.

Why We Don't Pray with Hopeful Expectation

One reason prayers seem to go unanswered is because of our own unbelief. We have no hopeful expectation that God will do anything. We may pray, but we really don't expect God to answer. During these times, we doubt His willingness or even His ability to intervene in our specific circumstances.

There are also times when we don't feel like we deserve anything good from God because of our Independent, Rebellious nature. I've felt this way many times. In my shame, I felt unworthy of even approaching God.

When considering our own Independence, our autonomous nature can also make us reluctant to follow what seems nonsensical. It's difficult to have *hopeful expectation* when the answer to our prayers doesn't seem to make sense. In times like these, we have a tendency to doubt God, ourselves, and may eventually undermine God's answer to our prayers through our own Independent ways.

Another reason we may not expect an answer to our prayers—let alone a miracle—is due to an inclination that God is an unapproachable cosmic being. He's way out there in the cosmos somewhere, and we're just a speck amongst many specks. As such, we wonder if God could possibly be interested in our specific and individual lives.

Though I'm sure there are other reasons we don't pray—like Complacency—I want to address each of the reasons mentioned above, directly. First, however, know that the Bible simply says, **"Is anyone among you in trouble? Let them pray..."** (James 5:13a, NIV).

❖ **Unbelief**

Believing and Trust are almost synonymous. Trust seems to carry a more weighted understanding of God's love, kindness, and genuine concern for our individual lives. However, believing—for many people—requires seeing.

Consider the wind. Can you see it? You may be able to see the results of a breeze blowing, but the wind itself is invisible to the human eye. Perhaps that's why the author of Hebrews tells us that believing is not about seeing; it's about having a *hopeful expectation*.

> "Faith is confidence in what we hope for and *assurance about what we do not see*" (Hebrews 11:1, NIV, *emphasis mine*).

There's a story in the Bible (found in Mark 9:14-29) where a man hadn't seen any results from Jesus' disciples concerning the healing of his son from an evil spirit. His son had been rendered mute and was often thrown into violent seizures by this demonic possession.

Jesus wasn't present, but had given His disciples the power and authority to heal people and drive out demons. Even so, their efforts yielded no results in healing this man's son. As such, the man's belief had been diminished.

Then, Jesus shows up! Upon asking what the problem was, the man described what had been going on and how Jesus' disciples had been unsuccessful in healing his son. Then the man says something that displays his lack of belief. He says to Jesus, "But *if* you can do anything, take pity on us and help us" (Mark 9:22b, NIV, *emphasis mine*).

Notice the man says, "IF" you can. Listen to the conversation that follows as Jesus questions the man's belief by asking the equivalent of "What do you mean IF I can?"

> "'If you can?' said Jesus. 'Everything is possible for one who believes.' Immediately the boy's father exclaimed, 'I do believe; *help me overcome my unbelief!*'" (Mark 9:23-24, NIV, *emphasis mine*).

What a beautiful prayer: *"Help me overcome my unbelief!"* We need to be real with God at *all* times. He already knows our hearts (see Psalm 139:1-4), so why try to fake your way through a prayer? Simply tell God that you're struggling to believe that He will—or even wants to—help. Ask Him to strengthen your faith and encourage your heart. If your heart is open and you truly desire the grace of Trusting Him more, God will come to your Rescue.

If you find it hard to believe without seeing, pray anyway. Pray for God to forgive your unbelief. Then pray from your heart. Pray whatever is on your mind and ask God to encourage your spirit and give you *hopeful expectation* in response to your heartfelt prayer. Being honest with God in asking for His help is the best way to *see* an answer to your prayers.

❖ Undeserving

As I reflect on my life, especially my prayer life, I notice a puzzling pattern (pattern puzzle). When I have been defiant in my actions, I often feel like I can't talk to God. Like I don't deserve anything good from Him because of my Rebellious ways. It's during these times that I notice that I rarely pray or don't pray at all.

If you find yourself in a place of Independence or all out Rebellion against God's best laid plans for your life, take a Selah (pause) and ask for help. It's during these times that our mayday prayers are most needed. When life is full of Trouble—especially by our own doing—God is waiting for us to take a pause, consider Him, and ask for His help.

When I married my third wife, I had been out of church, wasn't praying, and I wasn't reading the Bible—not even the shortest of devotions I received daily through email. I felt like my years of Rebellion had disqualified me, somehow, from even deserving a relationship with God.

Truth be told, none of us *deserve* anything from God. We have all sinned and have missed the mark of who God wants us to be and what God wants us to do (see Romans 3:23). The grace of God, however, extends far beyond our faults and defiance. The Bible says that when we come to faith in Jesus Christ, our Rebelliousness is forgiven and our slate is wiped clean forever.

> "Therefore, there is now no condemnation for those who are in Christ Jesus" (Romans 8:1, NIV).

> "For I will forgive their wickedness and will remember their sins no more" (Hebrews 8:12, NIV, *emphasis mine*).

> "He has removed our sin as far as the east is from the west" (Psalm 103:12, NLT).

Do you know why the wording for the last verse is specific to "east from the west" rather than "north from the south"? If you travel north—and continue traveling north—our spherical globe will eventually send you south again. As such, the north and the south meet at some point around Santa's house. But, if you travel east, you will never—ever—end up going west. If you have placed your faith in Jesus Christ, God has removed your sins—past, present, and future—so far from His sight, that your sins will never meet His condemnation. They can't. You are forgiven.

That's what my third wife lovingly and consistently demonstrated to me, every day, until I finally came around and gave God a chance again. It took me a while to begin true healing, but this wonderful woman showed me that—even though I had been on a Rebellious track for so long—God still loved me, still cared about my future, and just wanted me to come close to Him again.

The same is true for you. No matter how far you've gone, God's loving, grace-filled arms are just a U-turn away. And, when we turn to Him in true Surrender, we can be assured His ears are open to our Troubled needs. He loves you and—just like a loving Father—He longs for intimate conversations with His children, even when we've wandered far from the path He's chosen for our best.

❖ Reluctancy

There have been many times in my life when I've asked for the impossible. In many of those cases, what I was prompted to do by God wasn't easy.

I remember being in the hospital with a family on one such occurrence. A young boy had started attending our Wednesday evening ministry for kids, but his parents didn't seem to have any desire for God or the church. It seemed they were dropping their little boy off at church on Wednesday nights just to have some downtime from being parents.

After the boy had been coming to church for several months, his mother was diagnosed with a rare form of cancer. A tumor, the size of a small watermelon, had attached itself to her adrenal gland. She needed immediate surgery.

If recollection serves me right, at the time there were only two doctors in the world who had been successful with the surgical procedure she needed. She and her family went to Chapel Hill, North Carolina in hopes that one of these doctors could repeat their success.

I traveled the distance to be with the family during the surgery. On the morning of the surgery, I prayed with the boy's mom and the family members who were there. Many of the extended family are Christians, so we all came into bold, prayerful agreement that the surgery would go well, without any complications.

It didn't.

At some point during the surgery, one of the surgeons came out and said that the woman's liver was bleeding. The doctor told the family that the surgical team had been unsuccessful in getting the bleeding to stop, that they would continue to do everything they could, but that the future looked bleak.

Immediately the family went into a panicked frenzy. Every word that came out of their mouths was related to the doctors' abilities; but, God was never mentioned.

I walked away from the family and found the hospital's chapel. There, I got on my knees and prayed. I prayed fervently, with an aching heart. I prayed and prayed. I prayed right up to the moment I received a prompting from God that made me feel uneasy, fearful, dreadful, and reluctant. I felt as though I was supposed to confront the family about their faith and I knew my words might not be well received.

With a dreadful fear in my heart I went back, found the family, and gathered them together. Unsure how they'd receive the bold message God had given me to speak, God gave me peaceful assurance as I spoke the words I felt had been placed on my heart to say.

I told the family that in the early morning hours—and for the many hours of surgery preceding the doctor's grim prognosis—they had proclaimed faith in God. I went on to say that their faith had been displaced. I said that they were focused on what the surgeons couldn't do and not on what God was capable of doing. I boldly asked them where their faith was going to stand.

When I told the family they needed to choose between trusting the doctors and Trusting God, this is the banner of Truth I stood beneath:

> "...Be strong and courageous. Do not be afraid; do not be discouraged, for the Lord your God will be with you wherever you go" (Joshua 1:9b, NIV).

I wasn't sure how my boldness would be received, but God had given me directions. As I followed God's prompting—instead of my own fear—it was as if the whole family had been awakened from a slumber. As they heard me speak the Truth over their lack of faith, their hearts were convicted and encouraged at the same time.

Immediately, we huddled together and prayed boldly for a miracle. And a miracle was exactly what we received!

We'd barely gotten the word "Amen" out of our mouths when a surgical nurse appeared from behind the doors of the operating room and said the bleeding had stopped. The nurse went on to say they weren't sure what had caused the bleeding to stop, but we knew.

What a miracle! We all knew it was. But the best was yet to come.

When the mom had recovered, both she and the dad of the little boy they once dropped off for free babysitting began coming to church. And, not long after that, they both came to faith in Jesus Christ and were baptized.

Sometimes we can be hesitant to pray big prayers with hopeful expectation. And, often, when we do, we can be disinclined to follow through. In the case of this family, it was the fear of what others would think of me that almost made me buckle under the selfish pressure of pride. I don't even want to consider what may have happened if I had not been faithful to what God had directed me to do.

❖ *Nonsensical*

What do you do when the answer to your prayers surpasses fearful or dreaded action and crosses over into the nonsensical realm? Sometimes, in answer to our prayers, God may ask us to do things that just don't make sense.

There's a story in the Bible (found in 2 Kings 5) of a man named Naaman. He was a very powerful man, commanding the King's army in Aram. God had given him many victories over his enemies. But, there was one weakness about him. He suffered from a debilitating skin disease called leprosy.

He was told by one of his servants that a prophet in Israel—Elisha—had been given power by God to heal; so, Naaman packed supplies and set off to find this healer. Upon arriving at Elisha's house, instead of Elisha coming out himself, he sent a messenger out to this powerful leader with directions to dip himself in the Jordan river—seven times—and he would be healed. At first, Naaman was enraged because

Elisha didn't come out to meet him in person, call on His God, and wave his hands over him like a magician. He was also indignant toward the instructions of being *cleansed* in the Jordan River, as the Jordan was a very dirty river. He insisted there were greater rivers in which to wash himself if this were to be the means by which he'd be healed.

The Bible says that Naaman's servants approached him with a suggestion. According to the wording of the verse, they must have also been his friends, because they confronted this great leader with conviction.

> "'My father, if the prophet had told you to do something great, would you not have done it? How much more, then, when he tells you 'Wash and be cleansed!'" So he went down and dipped himself in the Jordan seven times, as the man of God had told him, and his flesh was restored and became clean like that of a young boy" (2 Kings 5:13-14, NIV).

Can you imagine what the end result would have been if Naaman hadn't followed God's nonsensical direction? What if he dipped himself six times, decided the treatment was ludicrous, and stopped there? But Naaman did the irrational thing. He dipped himself seven times and was healed.

Sometimes, God will prompt us—in our hearts or through another person—to take an illogical action in response to our prayers. Even so, our obedience (Surrender) to God is where healing and answered prayers take shape.

I'm the perfect example of responding to the illogical. I felt very strongly that God was calling me to write this book. Yet, every evening, when I got home from work, I was so physically exhausted that I didn't feel like writing.

So I began to pray. Every day—several times a day—I prayed for a solution. I knew this book had to be written. I knew it would change *my life* as I wrote it and I had been praying that it would greatly impact the lives of many others.

The answer I sensed was that I needed to quit my job, find something part-time, less physical, and utilize the rest of my time to share the inspiration God was giving me. The answer seemed nonsensical. I have bills to pay, groceries and gas to buy, and I have a daughter that I support financially in every way I can.

The pay from my current job provided for more than enough for me. It paid my bills, with a little pocket-change for extra expenditures. Following God's purpose for my life would cost me a lot of money. Still, I Trusted Him and His ability to provide for my needs. So, I took a leap of faith and quit my job in order to document the inspiration God was giving me.

Sure, things have been difficult. Money is tight and I've had to depend on family a couple of times to get me out of some stringent moments of need. But, I'm writing, God is providing, and I haven't felt better a day in my life since I made the choice to follow God's nonsensical answer to my prayers.

❖ *Unapproachable?*

As with unbelief, our hopeful expectation of answered prayers can often be limited by our inadequate understanding of God. We can't see Him, have heard He lives in the heavens somewhere, and can often feel Him to be distant and impersonal—even unapproachable.

Have you ever met someone famous or highly regarded and found them to be very down to earth. I have. Through various contacts and some impromptu meetings I've come into contact with some extremely influential people who took the time to actually have a meaningful conversation with me.

Not all renowned people are like that, but some are. The ones who truly care—though they may be people of great influence, or even every-day Joes—are more concerned about others than they are about themselves. As good as that sounds, these giving people are still a dim reflection of what God is like. In fact, God cared so much about us that He chose to take on a human, bodily form—as Jesus—and walk the earth with us, caring for the needs of everyone who came to Him with a sincere heart. That's compassion. That's personable. That's not a God who is distant or unapproachable.

God cares so much about us that the Bible says He knows how many hairs are on each of our heads (see Matthew 10:29-31), He saves every tear we've ever cried in a bottle (Psalm 56:8), and has adopted us as His very own children. As His children, we are told we can now call Him "Abba Father," which means *daddy* or *papa* (see Galatians 4:1-7).

God cares more for you than He does His own life. He sacrificed Himself—in the form of Jesus—on a cross as a ransom to redeem your very soul from the punishment we all deserve. He did this so we can spend an eternity with Him as our loving, compassionate, and very personable *dad*.

The next time you feel like God is a distant, cosmic being who is not interested in your personal life, talk to Him like you would a caring Father. Let Him know your needs and Trust that He cares about every moment of every day of your life.

Here are some verses to encourage you as you seek to know our very personable God:

"Come close to God and God will come close to you" (James 4:8a, NLT).

"The Lord is close to all who call on him, yes, to all who call on him in truth" (Psalm 145:18, NLT).

"...casting all your cares [all you anxieties, all your worries, and all your concerns, once and for all] on Him, for He cares about you [with deepest affection, and watches over you very carefully] (1 Peter 5:7, AMP).

What and How to Pray

One reason we don't pray or are hesitant to pray—which we didn't discuss in the previous section—is one I believe many Christian believers struggle with when it comes to approaching God in *hopeful expectation* tthrough prayer. Often our hesitancy is because we feel like we don't know *what* to pray or even *how to pray. Many times we don't even know where to begin*.

❖ ***Pray Like You're Talking To Your Best Friend***

I've heard some beautifully eloquent prayers in my life. Many of them were heartfelt. I knew those words had reached the throne room of heaven and God was listening intently. But, our words don't have to be eloquent; they just have to be sincere.

I once was a part of a very intimate group of men who met every Wednesday evening for years. We studied the Bible together, read Christian literature together, ate breakfast on Saturday mornings together, kept in contact with each other throughout the week, and definitely *prayed* for each other.

On Wednesday evenings, we always met around a campfire. Even when weather was inclement, we huddled inside a basement around a fake, battery-powered campfire that lit up and had little pieces of cloth that flapped as air was releases from the base of the unit. At the end of the meeting, we always shared prayer requests. Then we prayed around the circle for the person next to us and, often, for our own needs.

We kept our conversations with God real as we prayed around that campfire. I remember one time when one of my friends was praying and said, "God I'm struggling to keep my hands off myself."

We all had our heads bowed while he was praying, but when those words came out of his mouth, everybody looked up at once and glanced around. It was like we were all wondering the same thing at the same time. At the moment, we were all asking ourselves if it was really okay to talk to God like that. Then we all bowed our heads again as he finished praying.

That kind of prayer may seem shocking to you. The fact that I used his confession as an illustration may seem a bit off-putting to some. But His prayer was genuine, unfiltered, and conversational with God. He had a need and put it the best way he could.

That is exactly how we all should pray. God already knows our hearts. He knows our personalities, our normal way of speaking, and He's not offended when we come to Him with wounded hearts and raw words. He'd rather us be real than spout off eloquent, but empty, words.

Just talk to God. Speak to Him as you would your closest friend. Instead of worrying about *what* to say, simply try having a *normal conversation* with God today. Talk to Him about whatever is holding you back, whatever is imprisoning you, whatever your need or worry is. He's listening.

❖ Pray About Everything

There's not much I don't pray about. I pray for my own needs, my family's needs, and for people I know who are in need of God's intervention. I pray for safe travels and for traffic lights to change when I'm pressed for time. I pray every time I see an emergency vehicle with its lights flashing. In fact, as I'm writing this, a fire truck just drove by with its siren's blaring. I paused for a moment and asked God to minister to the needs of those involved and asked Him to let them know—deep down—that He is by their side.

I also pray short prayers of *thanks* for things like sunsets and blooming trees. I thank God each time I get to have a midweek lunch date with my daughter at school, which often includes takeout from Cracker Barrel (she loves their dumplings). I also thank God each time I get an encouraging word from someone, when I see God at work around me, or when He blesses me—whether in big or small ways.

Today, I prayed a short prayer of thanks for something small that could have turned out to be big if God wasn't looking out for me. I was driving distracted. When I looked up, there was a stop sign no less than ten feet away. I slammed on the brakes and came to a skidding halt. All of my belongings in the front and back seats shifted forward into the floorboards. At the same time, I heard the roar of a diesel truck as it whizzed through the intersection in front of me. In that moment—though everything I had in the car was scattered throughout—my prayer was a simple and short "Thank You, God."

All day long, as things pop in my head, instead of pondering the implications or worrying, I pray. There's nothing too big or too small that God doesn't care about (see Matthew 19:29 and Matthew 10:29), so I pray about everything.

The best way to enter into the *Sweet Spot* of God is to become intimate with Him through conversational prayer. Not just in the morning or at night or before mealtimes, but at *all* times. The Bible says that we are to "...pray without ceasing" (1 Thessalonians 5:17, ESV).

You may ask, "I barely pray now; how am I supposed to pray without ceasing?" It's easy. Just pray about everything—whether worries, struggles, or simply indications of thanks.

> "Pray in the Spirit on at *all* times and on *every* occasion..."
> (Ephesians 6:18, NLT, *emphases mine*).

❖ Check Your Motives

When I was a child, I had no concept of unity or division within the local church. I grew up Baptist. I knew there were other denominations, but didn't really know what that meant. I just knew if we got out early, we could beat the Methodists to our favorite lunch spot.

In my early twenties, however, I had gained some knowledge of why all churches weren't the same, and wanted to know more. My curiosity made me want to explore each of the Christian denominations. So, I decided to test drive a few.

I visited a Presbyterian, Lutheran, Methodist, Episcopal, Church of God, Adventist, and a Catholic Church. I also went to a non-denominational and an interdenominational church (which were just becoming popular back then).

One of the last churches I visited on my exploratory journey was another Baptist church. This one was different from the one I had attended most of my life, in that it was predominantly attended by African Americans. It was at this church that I heard a great Biblical truth taught in a way I'd never heard before. In just a few words, a commonly quoted verse suddenly made sense to me.

I've often heard people quote the end of James 4:2, "You do not have because you do not ask God" (NIV). Another version says "Ye have not because Ye ask not" (KJV). This is a verse many people have misused over the years. The presumption is that if I really need something, I should ask for it. And, that part is true. But the imposed meaning—by many people—assumes we don't have certain things in life because we haven't prayed and asked God for them.

That's just not true! I can't tell you how many times I've asked God to let me win the lottery. Guess what? I've asked, but it's *never* happened.

The difficulty in quoting that snippet of Scripture is the context in which it's written. The pastor at the last church I visited—in my early quest to understand the church—said the reason most of us don't win the lottery is because God knows we'd be on an exotic beach somewhere, sipping drinks with a tiny umbrella sticking out of the glass next Sunday instead of being at church. And, though that may or may not be true for you, the emphasis of that short statement took into consideration the context of *"you have not because you ask not."*

> "...You don't have what you want because you don't ask God for it. And even when you ask, *you don't get it because your motives are all wrong—you want only what will give you pleasure"* (James 4:2c-3, NLT, emphasis mine).

Before praying and asking God for what you perceive to be a need, ask yourself what motives are behind your request. Are you the only one—or the primary one—who will benefit from the answer to your prayer? Who else will be affected if God comes through in the way you've asked?

Do you find yourself praying mostly for yourself, and rarely for others? What's your motive?

In their devotional book for couples, *It Takes Two to Tango*,[20] by Gary and Norma Smalley, the authors consider what emotions or feelings are often the root of worry or fear. Listed among the causes of stress and anxiety are concerns over the future, your reputation, financial issues, property or possessions, time constraints, and adverse health issues. These are all things God wants us to talk to Him about through intimate prayer. The question becomes, why are these things causing us stress? And, is the answer we're asking for a genuine solution or a selfish resolve that requires no effort on our end?

Asking God to protect your reputation when you keep acting in unethical, demeaning, or irresponsible ways is not going to get the answer you're seeking. The same is true with your finances. Asking God to help you win the lottery so you can get out of debt—while impulse shopping for the latest fashion statement or technology device and putting it on your credit card—won't make you a millionaire.

As I consider the aforementioned passage and my own prayers, I think about when I asked God to heal my finger. Sure, there were selfish motives. It hurt, and I wanted it to stop hurting. I injured myself; God didn't do it. And, injuries like these take time to heal. But I wanted immediate results, and that's how I prayed.

Writing this chapter caused me to reflect on my prayer for my broken finger. In retrospect, I asked God to heal my finger, with immediacy, because of the pain (selfishness). But I also prayed because I couldn't write without the use of that finger and I knew God had purposed me to get the message of learning to live in His *Sweet Spot* written and delivered to the masses. My motives weren't for my own pleasure or enabled by selfish ambition. I knew I had a God-given task to accomplish, and I needed help in moving forward. As such, God answered my prayer.

I don't believe, however, that the James 4 passage is as concerned with the protection of our reputation, control over our spending habits, or the reasons we desire healing as it is about our self-seeking tendencies. James is very specific to say, "you only want what will give you pleasure" (v.3, NIV). James introduces this concept and concern just a few verses prior by saying, "But if you harbor bitter envy and selfish ambition in your hearts, do not… deny the truth" (James 3:14, NIV). He goes on to say, "For where you have envy and selfish ambition, there you find disorder and every evil practice" (James 3:16, NIV). My translation of "disorder and every evil practice" is "Trouble and Rebellion."

These are the practices we're trying to escape and avoid as we seek to live in *God's Sweet Spot*. So, the next time you pray, pause and reflect (Selah-Vie) on why you are asking God for specific answers to your prayers. Consider the impact your desired answer will have on others—if any—and proceed with humility and Godly purpose in your conversation with God.

❖ *Pray for God's Absolute Best*

I have an acute sense when it comes to prayer that is quite unusual. There are times when people ask me to pray about something and I get an immediate sense that whatever their circumstances—usually health related—will turn out okay. When things are sure to turn out the way in which the request for prayer has been asked, I know immediately. In those times, it's almost as though I know I don't even need to pray about the specific need. But, I do. And it always turns out to be the way I expected.

When I don't get an immediate sense about the circumstances, this doesn't mean healing isn't going to take place or the circumstances won't be resolved. I simply know I need to focus my attention on praying God's perfect will and purposes to be achieved through the situation at hand.

One such occasion, when I simply knew things would be okay, a loved one had recently been charged with assault. Her boyfriend had beaten her up, she had him arrested, and the police filed charges. Unfortunately, they also filed charges against her because he had scratches and scrapes on him as well—even though the wounds were defensive in nature.

When I learned of this event, I was asked to pray the charges would be dropped against her. I was told she was getting the best lawyer that could be afforded, but that there was some concern the abusive boyfriend would try to make her out to be the culprit.

Immediately, I had *that* sense. I knew the charges would be dropped and things would turn out for her best. I did pray the charges would be dropped; but, the overwhelming majority of my prayers for this young lady became focused on her finding a better way to live, clearly discovering God's purpose and plan for her life, and for her to have the courage to follow God's leading. That is still my prayer for her today.

In the previous section on checking your motives in prayer, I mentioned our tendencies to pray for the fulfilment of our own pleasures and selfish ambitions. The polar opposite of asking with selfish ambition, envy, or to satisfy personal longings is to *ask God for His absolute best outcome*—even if it doesn't coincide with our best laid plans.

> "This is the confidence we have in approaching God: that if we ask anything *according to his will*, he hears us. And if we know that he hears us—whatever we ask—we know that we have what we asked of him" (1 John 5:14-15, NIV, *emphasis mine*).

Earlier I mentioned situations when I don't have a specific sense related to how a particular prayer will be answered. When the *sense* isn't there, my immediate response is to *focus my attention on praying God's perfect will and purposes to be achieved through the situation at hand*. But how do we discern God's will in any particular circumstance or need?

As you'll discover during your Spiritual growth process, the Bible has an answer for almost everything. Some answers are very clear. Others may not be as obvious. When specificity for your circumstances is not apparent, the best course of action is not always found in asking your friends for advice—unless their guidance is based on Scripture. The best step is to turn to Scripture for answers, because, even when our needs are not specifically addressed in the Bible, the general concepts, direction, and assertions for changes in our heart attitudes are distinct throughout God's written Word.

> "*Don't copy the behavior and customs of this world*, but *let God transform you* into a new person *by changing the way you think*. Then you will learn to *know God's will for you*, which is good and pleasing and perfect" (Romans 12:2, NLT, *emphases mine*).

The way we experience perfect and pleasing changes in our lives is by altering the way we think. By Trusting what the *Word* says, not what the *world* says.

Yes, this means you need to start reading and studying the Bible—God's written Word and manual for life. Sometimes it's hard to get started because we think it's too difficult to understand.

Though we'll talk more about the importance of reading and knowing God's Word in another chapter, for now—especially if you have difficulty understanding the Bible—I'd suggest getting a translation of the Bible that is in a common vernacular, rather than old English. I'd suggest the New Living Translation (NLT) as a place to start.

For some, beginning a regular Bible reading routine may sound like a *drastic measure*, especially if all you want—or need—right now is to begin taking *baby steps*. Baby steps are great! If delving, head-first, into the Bible seems a bit intimidating, but you know you need Biblical principles to guide you in specific situations, I have a suggestion. One step I'd recommend when a need or a Troubling circumstance comes your way and you truly desire Godly wisdom is to use your favorite search engine and "Google it."

Whatever the situation, search for the answer online. My STRONG caution, however, is to always add the word "Scripture" or "Bible verse" to your search. Otherwise, you may only get the world's advice instead of the Word's best direction.

An example of this would be someone struggling with loneliness. Simply use your favorite search engine and type "loneliness Bible verses." I just did this exact search and got 2,560,000 results. How many of those results were actually based on the Bible, I'm not sure. But, in scanning the first couple of pages, most of what I found was solid, Biblical wisdom when it comes to loneliness.

When you find verses that relate to your present need, write each one on an index card. I have a whole stack of cards I turn to on a day-to-day basis. They keep me grounded and encouraged. They also help me discern God's will. And, as such, *they provide me with the ability to pray according to God's best purposes, know that He hears me when I pray, and know that His answer is forthcoming* (see 1 John 5:14-15).

The best part is that God always comes through on the promises He makes in His Word—when asked with humility and proper motives. The Bible says that when it comes to God's Word, one of His angels' primary responsibilities is to carry out what He has spoken. So, when we humbly pray—with God's purposes in mind—His angels spring into action.

> "Bless the Lord, you His angels, you mighty ones who do His commandments, *obeying the voice of His word!*" (Psalm 103:20, AMP, *emphasis mine*).

When your heart and motives are right, use your vocal cords to pray God's Word and absolute best over your circumstances. Voice the Word of God, aloud, and wait with *hopeful expectation* for God and His angels to respond.

❖ **Humble Yourself**

Years ago, a pastor told me to take a particular area of my life to the *cross* and lay it down. Specifically, he instructed me to find a place in my home and designate it as "The Cross." He even suggested placing a symbol of the cross in that chosen area. He then coached me to take my particular burden to the cross every time it reared its ugly head. Further indications were that I was to get on my knees and pray to God, *"I have carried this burden for too long. I am not capable of enduring the weight it's bringing on me. I give it to You, God, and Trust You to take it from me. In Jesus name, set me free; amen."*

This pastor told me to stay on my knees, in prayer, repeating the prayer over and over—with specificity—until I sensed God's peace over my present need. Furthermore, every time I felt spiritually attacked in this area, I was to get back on my knees and pray again—even if that attack occurred as I stood up from my initial prayer.

I understand some people are not physically able to get on their knees. If you *are* able, however, *do it*. Getting on your knees is an act of humility before God. It's an act of Surrender. And we know that Surrender is required before a true Rescue becomes formative in our lives.

Sometimes, however, we can't escape to our homes and our designated cross to pray. Perhaps we are tempted, tried, or find ourselves in desperate need when we're not at home in our place of Surrender. What then?

The answer goes back to the concept of *praying without ceasing* (see 1 Thessalonians 5:17). Wherever you are—in your car, at work, school, the gym, or at the grocery store—there's always time, if you choose to make it, to pause (Selah) and pray.

I gave up my job in order to spend time writing this book. I feel the concepts of what you're reading are inspired by God and believe it to be my current purpose in life to get these instructions for *Learning to Live in God's Sweet Spot* written, published, and into the hands of people who desperately want to see positive changes in their lives. However, I only have a short time to complete the book before I run out of money. As such, to supplement my income to be able to buy groceries while I'm writing, I started delivering food from restaurants for one of the major companies who supply this service.

A problem that has arisen from this means of provision is road rage. Not that I get furious and act like a madman, but I tend to say things to people in cars in front of me—who can't hear me—that are not reflective of God's heart and love.

So, before I get in my car to start my scheduled delivery times, I get on my knees and pray God will help me have a positive attitude and aid me in taming my tongue. Then, throughout the day, as I get aggravated and start my muted instructions on how other people should drive, I pause and pray. I ask God for forgiveness for the words or thoughts that just rampaged through my lips or head, and ask for His help in having a better attitude that reflects His heart, rather than my impatience.

The next time you feel down and out, tempted, oppressed, are in Trouble, or have a specific need, humble yourself before God, Surrender yourself and your circumstances to Him and pray. He promises to be with you:

> "I dwell on the high and holy place, but also with the contrite and *humble in spirit* in order to revive the spirit of the humble and to revive the heart of the contrite [overcome with sorrow for sin]" (Isaiah 57:15b, AMP, *emphasis mine*).

❖ Pray For Others

> "Do nothing from selfishness or empty conceit [through factional motives, or strife], but with [an attitude of] humility [being neither arrogant nor self-righteous], regard others as more important than yourselves. Do

not merely look out for your own personal interests, but also for the interests of others" (Philippians 2:3-4, AMP).

One way to humble yourself before God and clear your conscious of selfish ambition is to pray for other people and their needs. Praying for others also takes your mind off your own concerns, enabling you to put your needs in perspective.

Additionally, as you pray unselfish prayers for others, you'll begin to see the fruit of your conversations with God, allowing you to document and remember the faithfulness of His response to your prayers. Using whatever *monument* you've set up to remind you of God's love and kindness will solidify His goodness and memorialize His faithfulness (see the section on *A MONUMENTAL Event* in the chapter "Here I AM to Save the Day" for more on creating your monument).

Praying for others might seem overwhelming, especially if your own soul is depleted and you desperately need God's intervention. But we're going to take *Baby Steps* that will get you in the habit of praying humbly and selflessly.

I have absolute faith you'll see God at work when you choose to be obedient to God's command to pray for others (see 1 Timothy 2:1), by taking these simple steps:

1) Make a list of the people you care most about—including family, coworkers, friends, etcetera;

2) Next to each name, write a short description of any area you are aware, in which they have a need (of any sort). If you're unaware of a particular need, you may consider asking them. Or, you can just leave that part blank;

3) Get seven notecards. On each card, write a day of the week (Monday-Sunday);

4) Evenly distribute the names of the people you listed on each card, along with the short description of their need;

5) Keep the cards in a confidential, but accessible place;

6) Each morning when you get up, go to the place you've designated to be your *Cross* and pray for the people on the card that coincides with that particular day of the week. Make sure you pray for these people *before* talking to God about your own needs;

7) And, pray for the people on that day's card at least three times during the day, setting a reminder on your phone (or other device) as a way of keeping yourself focused.

When I pray for others, I see dramatic results. I see frequent results. I see more answers to prayer when I pray for others than when I pray for myself. I believe the reason for this is because my prayers for others are not encumbered by selfish desires.

As I mentioned before, there will be times when you have no idea how to pray for someone on your list. Consider asking them what thing(s) make their day complicated. Then pray. People who need prayer often appreciate knowing someone is coming alongside them in the midst of their Troubles.

If you are uncomfortable asking, or believe a particular person on your list may be hesitant in responding, consider personalizing—by name—this simple, Biblical prayer. It's a powerful prayer for anyone in any circumstance.

> "I pray that from his glorious, unlimited resources he will empower you with inner strength through his Spirit" (Ephesians 3:16, NLT).

❖ *Be Confident*

When asking for wisdom, James 1:5-8 tells us that God gives His wisdom to anyone who asks in faith. James also tells us that God gives us His wisdom, without holding our faults against us. The condition, however, is that we ask for wisdom with the certainty that God will direct us and give us the determination to follow through, according to His guidance.

The same is true when it comes to prayer as it is with wisdom. Instead of praying "If you are willing," pray "I know you love me and want what's best for me. That's why I'm coming to you with my need" (or another person's need).

> "Let us then approach God's throne of grace *with confidence*, so that we may receive mercy and find grace to help us in our time of need" (Hebrews 4:16, NIV, *emphasis mine*).

Sometimes I doubt my prayers. I doubt I'm asking the right thing with the right motives. It's hard to have confidence (or, as some versions put it, "boldness") when we're unsure of what to pray. On these occasions, begin your prayer by asking God for wisdom in what to pray. Ask Him to show you His very best, instead of your doubtful longings. Then wait—with hopeful expectation—for God to prompt your heart with the kind of prayer you are confident in asking. When you have a better sense—through God's provision of wisdom—pray boldly and with confidence that your conversation with God is effectual in resolving the need at hand.

❖ Pray With Diligence

Earlier in the "Nonsensical" section of *Why We Don't Pray,* I made note of a powerful leader—Naaman—who needed healing from the terrible skin disease of leprosy. In order for him to be healed, he had to dip himself seven times in the Jordan River. I then posed the question, "What if he dipped himself six times, decided the treatment was ludicrous, and stopped there?"

When you don't sense God's immediate answer to your unselfish and confident prayers, don't give up before the miracle happens!

> "Ask and *keep on asking* and it will be given to you; seek and *keep on seeking* and you will find; knock and *keep on knocking* and the door will be opened to you. For everyone who keeps on asking receives, and he who keeps on seeking finds, and to him who keeps on knocking, it will be opened (Matthew 7:7-8, AMP, *emphases mine*).

Waiting for an answer to prayer is difficult, especially when the need seems to be critically urgent. Keep asking. Keep seeking. Keep knocking on the door to God's throne room. And, as a repeated theme you'll notice throughout this book, don't give up. Instead, *wait* with *hopeful expectation*.

You may recall my miraculous answer to my prayer for the healing of my index finger on my dominant, right hand. After over a week and a half of complete inability to use my first finger and excruciating pain when I dared trying to bend it, I prayed for God's healing so I could use it to continue writing and doing His work.

The very next day, I was able to bend my finger at least fifty percent of its normal flexibility. That day, I started using it to write again. Over the next several days, I continued to pray for healing. By day three I was able to grip the doorknob to open my front door—and, it's a very tight knob to turn. I continued to pray. By the end of day seven, I was finally able to make a fist.

I felt like Naaman. I didn't have to dip myself in the Jordan seven times, but it took seven days of continually asking, seeking, and knocking to be able to use my hand to do everyday tasks. If your conversations with God are not yielding answers—though sometimes the answer is "no" or "wait"—check your motives, ask God for wisdom, pray for His best outcome, keep praying, and wait with hopeful expectation on God to come through.

❖ *When You Don't Know What to Pray*

As you seek to grow in intimacy with God through prayer for others, for yourself, and with genuine thanks in your heart for what He's going to do, is doing, and has done, there will also be times when you find yourself at a total loss for words. Even after asking for wisdom, you may still find yourself not knowing what to pray and without clarity concerning what steps you should take moving forward. The hope we have in these situations is that God already knows our hearts, He knows our needs, He knows what's best, and He's provided a solution to our deficiency in knowing *what* or *how* to pray.

> "In the same way the Spirit [comes to us and] helps us in our weakness. We do not know *what* prayer to offer or *how* to offer it as we should, *but the Spirit* Himself [knows our need and at the right time] *intercedes on our behalf* with sighs and groanings too deep for words. And He who searches the hearts knows what the mind

of the Spirit is, because the Spirit intercedes [before God] on behalf of God's people *in accordance with God's will*" (Romans 8:26-27, AMP, *emphases mine*).

When you don't know how to pray during your conversations with God, it's always best to confess to God that you're not sure what you should be asking or how you should be praying. If this is the case, tell God you fully Trust Him to bring about His absolute best in the situation and thank Him, in advance for how He's going to work. God will recognize your humility and respond according to His perfect will in your situation.

Selah (Pause for Reflection)

Take *15 Minutes* and Make this Chapter *Personal*

NOTE: Always keep a Bible, notebook, and pen ready. ***Why?*** *I believe God will open himself up to you during this time of reflection, just as He does for me.*

I hope this chapter on prayer has strengthened your confidence, knowing God has a personal interest in your life. I pray this part of your journey has given you *hopeful expectation* in seeing answers to your prayers and will encourage you to prayerfully intercede for others more often than you do for your own needs. You will find it truly liberating to see your unselfish prayers answered.

Along your pathway to heartfelt and effective conversations with God, it's important to show your Trust in His best throughout the process. Thank Him for loving you enough to get involved in your life. Thank God for the answers He is in the process of providing. Be deliberate in thanking Him, again, as you begin seeing answers. And, consider adding each answer to your Monument (see "Here I AM to Save the Day" chapter as a reminder on finding a way to memorialize God's faithfulness in your life).

As you take a moment of reflective Selah, meditate on the following verse, dissecting each part and how it may pertain to your current prayer-life; then, claim its promise as a victory over every circumstance you encounter:

> "Trust in the Lord with all your heart and lean not on your own understanding; in all your ways submit to him, and he will make your paths straight [will direct your path]" (Proverbs 3:5-6, NIV, [bracketed] note mine).

Trusting God, in full Surrender to Him, is the most critical part. Realizing that our prayers can often be selfish and our expected outcome unrealistic—because we trust ourselves more than God—is just as important. Trusting God's answers and following His determined path is assurance of your Surrender. As you pray with humility and Surrender, the best is yet to come! God will direct you in everything you do!

Write the above verse on a notecard and carry it with you, everywhere you go, for the next seven days. Put the card in a place you access regularly each day—perhaps your wallet, pocket, purse, phone carrier, or tape it inside your laptop's open space. Each day, throughout the week, consider the implications and promises that are *yours* if you choose to live by God's Word rather than your or the world's ways.

As you consider the way you've always done it, in comparison to this reflective verse, keep a log of how often you seem to do your own thing, instead of asking God for His direction. Each time you catch yourself leaning on your own understanding, pause, pray, and change your course. The outcome will be far better than any of your own best laid plans. I promise!

Chapter Sixteen

WHO'S YOUR DADDY?

"I am writing to you, fathers, because you know him who is from the beginning. I am writing to you, young men, because you have overcome the evil one. I write to you, dear children, because you know the father.
~ 1 John 2:13-14a, NIV

Many people grow up without ever really knowing their biological father. All too often, children are abandoned by a father who decides to leave his family, leaving the mom—or other family members—to raise a child all alone. More often than not, it's the *system* that ends up with the father's rightful responsibility. In this case, some of these children are adopted by families and come to know a loving father. These are the few that find some sort of hopefulness. The saddest of fatherless children, however, are those whose father has never truly been present in their lives, even though they reside in the same house for years.

In my youngest years, our family didn't have much. My mom was working on climbing the ladder in her career, but hadn't made it there yet. My dad was a hard worker. Though he lost a job from time to time—once being my fault—he always did his best to provide for his family. They both did.

Sadly, my dad would come home exhausted from laborious jobs and didn't have the energy to invest time in my sister or in me. I never learned how to throw a baseball, rarely went fishing, never went hunting, and simply saw my dad as the enforcer of punishment during my childhood.

My dad has many regrets about his behavior and inaccessibility as a father and is now a very docile man who wishes he could change a lot of things and has prayed to forget much of his lamentable past. Unfortunately, his prayers seem to be answered, as he has developed Alzheimer's in his later years.

Don't you just wish you could change things at times? That moment? That decision? Those years? What if we could pick the parents we have? I'm sure our parents would like the same choice—at times—to pick the kind of kids they have.

Though none of us have those kinds of choices, we *do* have a choice in who we will call our spiritual father. We can either choose the love and grace of our Father in heaven—whom I call God—or we can choose to follow in the footsteps of the devil, who is referred to as the "Father of Lies" (see John 8:44).

Both choices offer distinguishable characteristics. Let's take a brief look at how some names each of these "fathers" are ascribed in the Bible and see which one seems like the Father we're cuddling with currently.

❖ **The Heavenly Father**

Generally, we speak of God the Father simply as God. In Hebrew, His name is YHWH (Yahweh). While reading through the Old Testament, when you see LORD in all caps, that's the English translation of YHWH.

There are also less specific names for God in the Bible. One example is "Lord," with only the first letter capitalized. The Hebrew term used for Lord is often Adonai, which means "master" or Elohim, which means "sovereign and mighty God." There are also cases when the term God is a preface to a description of Him. Some prefaces begin with name "El" (a general sense for the essence of God) and others begin with His formal name, Yahweh.

Here are a few examples of attributes given to God by the way He is addressed or described:

- El-Elyon: The most high God;
- El-Olam: The everlasting God;
- El-Roi: The God who sees everything;
- El-Chewl: The God of creation and giver of life;
- El-Deah: The God of knowledge and wisdom;
- Yahweh-Rapha: The God who heals;
- Yahweh-Jireh: The God who provides;
- Yahweh-Shalom: The God of peace.

Other names in the Bible, like "Prince of Peace," "Savior," and "Redeemer" all describe who our Heavenly Father is. They describe what He does and His infallible character.

❖ The Fallen Father

On the other hand, there is the "Father of Lies," who is the devil himself. There are also other names for the devil that give us an idea of his character.

- Abaddon: The Hebrew name for Satan, which means "destruction;"

- The Accuser: Accusing us, before God, of our wrong doings, trying to undermine God's grace toward us and blessings on us;
- Angel of Light: Deceiving people by pretending to be a source of light instead of darkness;
- Antichrist: Standing against everything Jesus is, does, and desires for His followers' lives;
- The Beast: Pretty self-explanatory;
- Beelzebub: Ruler of demons;
- The Enemy: Always attacking; always seeking to kill, steal, and destroy our livelihood;
- Roaring Lion: Ravenous, always seeing us as prey and our circumstances as an opportunity to devour us.

Though there are many other descriptive terms for the devil, the one that intrigues me most is the designation "Father of Lies." The devil lies to us. He whispers in our ears that we've made too many mistakes and that our current state is where we'll always dwell. He tells us God that is disappointed in us, always.

Recently, I messed up in a bad way. My disobedience in following God's best was deliberate, and I suffered the consequences. While delivering food for one of the major food delivery services, I backed into someone's mailbox. I didn't notice any real damage; so, I went about my next delivery. I should have gotten out of my car, surveyed the damage, and alerted the homeowner. I didn't.

Ultimately, a police report was filed, I was called to the scene, and I am awaiting estimates for repairs so I can make reparations. During the whole scenario, I was scared. I hadn't had any dealings with law enforcement since I was a teenager. The whole situation literally had me shaking.

I felt bad all day about not stopping to tell the homeowner, but truly figured it was just a bump. Still, I had prayed all day for forgiveness. Even though I prayed, I never felt a sense of peace. Then, when the police became involved, all I felt was fear. I felt fear for the consequences, but I also feared God.

What if this was the one time God chose not to extend grace and, instead, inflicted His wrath? What if the blessing I'd been praying about had been nullified by my self-preserving actions? I trembled at the thought.

Later in the evening I talked with a dear friend of mine and confessed my sin. She prayed with me over the phone. She affirmed God's forgiveness and His removal of my sin "as far as the east is from the west" in her prayer. She also rebuked the devil for whispering lies into my ears and my heart.

I felt peace, immediately, as my friend prayed concerning the blessing I'd been hoping would come to fruition. She prayed that if this opportunity was God's will for me, He'd walk with me into that season of my life. She knew I'd asked for forgiveness and was making restitution for my actions, so she prayed that if the answer to my prayer didn't turn out the way I wanted, God would open my eyes to the alternative plan He'd had for me all along. What a difference it makes to listen to God's Word and plan spoken over your life as opposed to believing the lies the devil imposes on us!

The Accuser and Liar had made me doubt God. He'd made me doubt myself. He'd told me lies that I had come into agreement with, instead of relaxing in the Truths and promises of God.

Making the Choice

The choice between an ever-present, all-knowing, gracious, and loving God and a fallen angel who pretends to show us an easier, better way—but is full of lies—seems to be an easy one. But, our actions don't always correspond with our intended choice.

> "Enter through the narrow gate. For wide is the gate and broad is the road that leads to destruction, and many enter through it. But small is the gate and narrow the road that leads to life, and only a few find it" (Matthew 7:13-14, NIV).

If you find yourself on the broad road and your actions are mostly Complacent, you're regularly Frustrated, act Independently from God—without seeking His direction in your everyday choices—or are in full-blown Rebellion, guess which father's hand you're holding the most. It's a hard pill to swallow, but many Christians listen more to the lies of the devil and follow the ways of the world rather than claiming the promises of God and following His Word.

If you have placed your faith in Jesus Christ as the only way to receive forgiveness for your sins, but find yourself doubting God's grace and goodness at times or find yourself on the broad road to Trouble, do what I did. Ask for forgiveness, seek Godly counsel, confess your sins, and pray with others for strength to overcome the evil schemes and lies of the devil. Pray for healing, deliverance, and for freedom (see James 5:13-16).

There are several questions we must each ask ourselves. Have I ever truly placed my absolute faith in Jesus and in God's grace? Do I truly Trust God? Do I truly desire to live a Surrendered life to Him?

When Jesus taught His disciples to pray in Matthew 6:9-13, He began by demonstrating how to approach God in prayer by saying "Our Father in heaven..." (verse 9, NIV). I know that the God of the Bible is *my* Father, but is He *OUR* Father? In essence, what I'm asking is "Who's *YOUR* Daddy?"

Absolute faith in Jesus and in God's grace is more than going to church or saying some rote prayer. It's not even about "believing" in God or Jesus. Don't you think that the devil believes in Jesus, believes that He died on a cross, and that He arose from the dead on the third day? The Bible says even the demons believe in God and tremble with fear (see James 2:19). For that matter, those of Jewish faith, Muslims, Hindus, and many other religions believe Jesus existed. His death and resurrection are historically recorded in other documents besides the Bible. Does that mean all of these people—including the devil and his demonic following—are heaven-bound?

If you have truly placed your faith in Jesus Christ to save you from the power of sin and death, it is not my intention to make you doubt your faith. If you aren't sure about your faith, however, I want you to truly consider where, and in whom, you are regularly placing your Trust.

The Bible is clear about what it takes to be saved. When an official of the Roman Empire asked what he must do to be saved, Paul and Silas—who had been jailed by this man—responded by saying, "Believe in the Lord Jesus and you will be saved..." (Acts 16:31, NIV). In every sense of the True Word of God, I believe this statement to be absolute. "Believing" in the Lord Jesus Christ is the only way to be saved. My question for you is what does it mean to "believe"?

The Bible has been translated into many languages, worldwide. It has also been translated into English with several different versions, all saying the same thing, but with differing terminology for each reader's ease. The Old Testament has been translated from the original Hebrew language, while the New Testament has been rendered from the original Greek and Aramaic.

When considering the best translation of each Hebrew, Greek, or Aramaic word, there are often various definitions for each word—much like there are different meanings for particular words in our own language. Since most Christians are not scholars in ancient languages, the translators do the best they can to determine—in context—which varying word to use in place of the original language. This is why I often turn to the Amplified Version of the Bible (AMP) or the AMPC (Amplified Bible, Classic Edition). Both use [brackets] to suggest other or deeper meanings the original language intended. Take a look at Acts 16:31 (mentioned above) in the Amplified Bible, Classic Edition (AMPC):

> "...Believe in the Lord Jesus Christ [give yourself up to Him, take yourself out of your own keeping and entrust yourself into His keeping] and you will be saved..." (Acts 16:31a, AMPC).

"Believing," therefore, is an act of Surrender. I believe the initial act of Surrendered faith seals your forgiveness and ensures your heavenly home. I also believe Surrender is something we do each and every moment of every day. Sure, there will be times of Complacency, Frustration, Independence, Rebellion, and Trouble. Just like my incident with the mailbox. Just like the history of God's people, the Israelites. Just like the history and cycle of all mankind. But, the sooner you recognize your pattern puzzle, Surrender, and cut your cycle short, the sooner you'll find yourself back in a place of Trust—*God's Sweet Spot*.

If you are unsure about your relationship with God, pray and ask God to give you insight. He wants nothing more than to have an intimate relationship with you. Here are some questions you may ask yourself:

- Do I believe my sinful, even Rebellious, nature goes against God's best plan for my life?
- Do I believe my actions are punishable?

- Since the Bible says my sin requires the punishment of death, do I believe Jesus' death paid the ransoming cost for my sins by dying on a cross in my place?
- Do I believe Jesus was raised from the dead to reveal the power of God over death and my sins?
- Am I willing to begin the process of Surrendering each area of my life—knowing I will make mistakes along the way—to God's best laid plan for me?
- Am I willing to learn to live according to God's will and instructions as laid out in His Word—the Bible?

If you answered yes to each of these questions, you may consider using the following model of prayer. It's just a model. What's most important is that you personalize the prayer with a sincere heart

> "Yahweh (God), I believe You to be the One True God. I confess I have made mistakes in my life. In fact, I've been downright Rebellious at times. I realize my Independent ways are deserving of punishment—even death and eternal separation from You. I believe Jesus died on a cross to pay the penalty for my sins. I believe He rose from the dead to reveal Your power over sin and death and to give me a new life. I ask you, today, to forgive me. I accept the grace You are offering me through the sacrifice of Your Son, Jesus. I will need Your help as I grow to be the person You've always planned for me to be. As such, I Surrender my life to You and ask for Your help in becoming all that You desire for my life. Prompt my heart—through Your Holy Spirit—when I am straying off course. Make clear to me Your ways and give me the courage and strength I need to follow You. Today I ask You to become my heavenly Father. In Jesus' name, I humbly ask these things; amen."

Who's Your Daddy?

If you just prayed that prayer—or have prayed a similar one in the past—with a Surrendered heart, you can now pray the Lord's Prayer (see Matthew 6:9-13), knowing that God is OUR Father in heaven. You can rest assured in knowing who your real Daddy is.

If, however, you're unsure you can answer each of the questions above in the affirmative, or need some help understanding the concepts of each question, seek the counsel of a Godly friend or pastor. Maybe you have questions about whether God even exists, whether there's an actual heaven or hell, or want to know what your purpose in life is. Reach out and ask other people you know who seem to have a growing relationship with God. I assure you, they will be happy to journey with you and help you find answers to your questions.

If you are an introvert or feel a bit intimidated by reaching out to someone for help, gotquestions.org is a great resource to get you started. This website literally has over a half-million answers to common questions people have about the Bible and faith. I personally use the site as a resource when I have looming questions. And, I usually find an answer. I believe you will too!

If the God of the Bible is already your Father, but you have not been acting like it, cut your cycle short. Call out to Him in Surrender. Release the hand of the devil and his worldly ways. Grasp tightly onto God's mighty right hand and begin living like a True son or daughter of "*Our Father in heaven.*"

The decision to place your faith in Jesus and Surrender your life to Him for the first time—or to give yourself fully to Him once again—is the best decision you'll ever make. If you're concerned about how to live a life of Surrender and how to stay in *God's Sweet Spot*, that's what the rest of this book is all about!

Selah (Pause for Reflection)

Take *15 Minutes* and Make this Chapter *Personal*

> *NOTE: Always keep a Bible, notebook, and pen ready.*
> ***Why?*** *I believe God will open himself up to you during this time of reflection, just as He does for me.*

For reflection on knowing the God of the Bible—our Father in heaven—as your True dad, consider the chorus from the song "Good, Good Father,"[21] as sung by Chris Tomlin:

> "You're a good, good Father;
> It's who You are; it's who You are; it's who You are
> And I'm loved by you;
> It's who I am; it's who I am; it's who I am."

God truly is a good, good Father. Confess His goodness, His love, and His faithfulness aloud right now. Then, come into agreement with God that you are loved—even cherished—by Him. Claim the fact that you are His. It's who you are, because of Who He is.

To take this time of reflection a bit further, even if you've heard the song before, take the initiative to look up the complete lyrics and read them–out loud—as though you were the one who'd written the song. I'd even encourage you to find the song on YouTube or your favorite music app and listen to the song two or three times. Listen to it in a solitary place where you can truly worship OUR good, good Father.

Chapter Seventeen

ATTITUDE OF GRATITUDE

"As we express our gratitude, we must never forget that the highest appreciation is not to utter words, but to live by them."
~ *John F. Kennedy*[22]

Do you know someone who suffers from panic attacks? Perhaps you have experience with this intense physical and emotional occurrence yourself. One that leaves you feeling depleted and defeated.

The experience of a panic attack varies and can be much worse than I've experienced. I can only describe how I have felt—in the past—when I experienced this horrifying and debilitating feeling. I could always feel my panic attacks coming on. The first indicator I usually felt was an overwhelming sense of anxiety. As the symptoms progressed, the next thing I would feel was in my chest. I felt as though my lungs were constricting. My heart would begin palpitating, my head would achingly pound, and I would feel like an elephant was sitting on my chest. I felt like I couldn't breathe. If I were conscious enough, I could force myself to breathe, but there were times all I could do was gasp. In my worst panic attacks, this tightening of my chest would make me think I was having a heart attack, which only heightened my anxiety, fear, and feelings of delusion.

After the panic attack, my body would simply go limp and I would be nonfunctional for hours.

The worst of my panic attacks—having at least three severe instances a week—continued for years, between 2004 and 2006. During this time, my doctor prescribed me three 1mg doses of Xanax a day (the blue ones). He would write me a three month prescription (90 pills) with three refills (this was back in the day when controlled substances weren't as regulated as they are today).

There were times when I needed three pills per day. But, there were other times when I would catch the attack at its onset and be able to ward it off with just a half of one pill.

After years of taking Xanax, and trying other anti-anxiety medications, my panic attacks came to a complete halt. They subsided right after my first wife and I separated. This was also during a season where I left a very stressful job. I don't know if the emotional intensity between my first wife and I caused the attacks or if the feelings of inadequacy in my job was the major contributor. All I know is that they suddenly stopped.

The attacks ceased for years—without *any* symptoms at all—until my third wife left me. Though I was not living a life fully Surrendered to God, I had grown in my understanding of God and decided to try something besides pharmaceuticals to relieve the symptoms.

I joined a group of people who had experienced comparable Frustrations and acted in similar Rebellious ways as I, but who were recovering from their losses, negative mindsets, and addictive traits. It was in this group I learned the concept of having an *Attitude of Gratitude*. The general concept is to learn to be grateful for even the smallest of things, the smallest steps toward a better life, and even for the things that had brought me to a place of desperation and localized Surrender.

We were encouraged to write a daily list, expressing thankfulness for both big and small blessings.

Considering all the challenges, Frustrations, and Troubles I've experienced in life, the most devastating—to this point—was when my third wife left me. I felt as though my life was no longer worth living. It was then that my panic attacks resumed. Putting into practice, however, what I was learning from this group of peers—who'd experienced much of what I was going though at varying points in their lives—I decided to begin focusing on the positives in life, rather than spending all my time dwelling on the negative consequences I was experiencing and could not change. Each time I sensed the onset of a panic attack, I would stop what I was doing and begin thanking God, aloud, for everything that came to my mind. If nothing came to mind, I forced myself to dig deeper and find the silver lining. I thanked God that I had a job, a place to live, food in my pantry, that I was alive and breathing. In that moment of feeling like my chest was beginning to constrict, I thanked God for the greatest and the smallest of things. The result? Within a matter of minutes of expressing an *Attitude of Gratitude* my chest would loosen and my anxiety would lose its control.

It's Who He Is And What He Does

In the Selah section of the last chapter, I asked you to reflect on the words from the song "Good, Good Father." Part of the chorus says, "It's who You are; It's who You are; It's who You are." Who God is, what He has done, is doing, and will do in our lives is the reason we celebrate Him through thanksgiving. As Jesus taught His disciples to pray, not only did He declare God to be "Our Father in heaven," who is a loving *dad*, He also references the reverential nature of God by saying "Hallowed be your name" (see Matthew 6:9, NIV).

In general, "hallowed" means to keep God's name uniquely set apart for worship, respect, and admiration. When we approach God in prayer, we are to humbly approach God, realizing who He is and who we are in comparison.

In today's society, respect is usually earned, rather than given. Though our reverence should be freely given to God, He's definitely earned it. Every day you breathe another breath, that respiratory function was given to you by God and that, alone, makes Him worthy of honoring Him with our attitudes and actions.

Maybe you're in a rut of Complacency, Frustration, Independence, Rebellion, or even Trouble. That's all the more reason to praise God and offer your thanks as a gift to Him. The Bible says that because of God's great love for us, He does not treat us as we deserve. Instead, His mercies toward us are renewed every day (see Lamentations 3:22-23). Because of who God is, the ultimate sacrifice He made to pay for our sins, and His continued mercies toward us, our attitudes should always be of gratitude. *Hallowed* be His name!

Benefits Of A Grateful Heart

It's amazing how turning our attention away from negative circumstances or feelings and toward the faithfulness of God can transform even our physical state. Expressing thankfulness to God, however, has so many more benefits than easing emotional anxiety or physical distress.

An *Attitude of Gratitude* helps us take our mind off ourselves and replaces those thoughts with a reminder that we're not in control. God is. Gratefulness reminds us we were never meant to be self-sufficient. Instead, God is our Provider (Yahweh-Jireh), and all good things come from Him (see James 1:17). In a place of humility and thanks, we realize our dependency on God and how much we truly need Him.

Reflecting on (Seleh) and remembering (monumentalizing) the goodness and faithfulness of God is a reverberating result of a grateful heart. When we memorialize God's faithfulness through thanksgiving, it helps us put future trials and Troubles in perspective. With a vivid memory of God's provision, healing, intervention, and Rescue from past circumstances, it becomes easier to Trust Him when faced with new uncertainties and praise Him—in advance—for His faithfulness to come.

In addition to the welfares already mentioned, one of the greatest benefits of expressing our gratefulness to God is not just a change of mindset. Instead, it is the advantage of actually seeing our circumstances beginning to change.

The Bible is very clear that we reap what we sow. In other words, what we plant is what grows. When our words and expressions are always filled with negativity, we reap undesirable lives and consequences. But, when the words we speak are positive, they are also life-giving. Which would you rather determine your future—words of life or words of death?

> "Death and life are in the power of the tongue, and those who love it and indulge it will eat its fruit and *bear the consequences of their words*" (Proverbs 18:21, AMP, *emphasis mine*).

As you journey in your faith discovery you will learn that even difficulties can become positive experiences—if you allow them to be. They can give you the ability to help others who are experiencing similar circumstances and—ultimately—bring greater thankfulness as you become more and more confident in God's faithfulness. Even if you can't see or imagine anything positive coming from your current situation, thank God anyway. Thank Him, despite your doubts or fears, because God's plan is always to bring good out of what appears to be uncertain, threatening, or even devastating.

Take just a moment and reread that last paragraph. Could these thoughts be pure speculation? Or, are they the Truths and Promises of God?

> "*All praise to God*, the Father of our Lord Jesus Christ. God is our merciful Father and the source of all comfort. *He comforts us in all our troubles* so that we can comfort others. When they are troubled, *we will be able to give them the same comfort God has given us*" (2 Corinthians 1:3-4, NLT, *emphases mine*).

> "*Let your roots grow down into him*, and let your lives be built on him. Then your faith will grow strong in the truth you were taught, *and you will overflow with thankfulness*" (Colossians 2:7, NLT, *emphases mine*).

> "...We know that God causes everything to work together for the good of those who love God and are called according to his purpose for them" (Romans 8:28, NLT).

Though there are many benefits and promises related to our expressed thankfulness toward God, there is one final thought I'd like you to consider. It's a question that may result in an impulsive "Yes," but I want you to truly consider the implications as it relates to having an *Attitude of Gratitude*—no matter the situation, trial, or Trouble. Here's the question: If the only answered prayer you were ever guaranteed was your prayer of Surrender for the forgiveness of your sins—through your genuine faith in Jesus Christ—would that be enough to have an eternally joyful heart of thankfulness toward God?

> "In all this you greatly rejoice, though now for a little while you may have had to suffer grief in all kinds of trials. These have come so that the proven genuineness of your faith—of greater worth than gold, which perishes even though refined by fire—may result in praise, glory and honor when Jesus Christ is revealed. Though you have not seen him, you love him; and even though you do not see him now, you believe in him and are filled with an inexpressible and glorious joy, for you are receiving the end result of your faith, the salvation of your souls" (1 Peter 1:6-9, NLT).

Thankfully, we don't have to make that choice! God loves us enough to forgive us AND to extend His *continued* grace, mercy, promises, and answers to our humble prayers.

Selah (Pause for Reflection)

Take *15 Minutes* and Make this Chapter *Personal*

> *NOTE: Always keep a Bible, notebook, and pen ready.* **Why?** *I believe God will open himself up to you during this time of reflection, just as He does for me.*

> "I will give thanks to you, Lord, with all my heart; I will tell of all your wonderful deeds" (Psalm 9:1, NIV)

As you consider all the things God has done, is doing, and promises to do in the future for your well-being, the following four *active* reflections will help cement your confidence in God, enable you to share your genuine Trust in God with others, and provide a prayer—directly from the Word of God and carried out by His angels—that reflects a heart of growing faith, an enlarged capacity for gratefulness, and hope for your future:

1) In a notebook or journal, each day for the next ten days, write down at least ten things for which you are thankful. Try not to repeat anything from a previous day's list. Keeping each day's list individualized will require some thought and reflection, which is what this section is all about (Selah). It will also provide you with a list of 100 things you are grateful for at the end of the ten days;

2) At the end of the ten days, make a total evaluation of God's faithfulness and consider how making the list each day has increased your overall attitude toward life and grown your faith. Make some notes to memorialize how you feel after spending ten days being intentionally thankful;

3) Then, go out on a limb—even if you are reluctant or feel intimidated—and share the concept of this exercise with someone

who may need some encouragement, making sure to emphasize the resulting change of mindset it's caused within you. Encourage this person to begin his/her own list and to let you know any changes noticed after spending ten days expressing an *Attitude of Gratitude*;

4) Finally, ponder the following prayer, personalize it, and pray these words for the person you shared this exercise with and over your own life:

"I pray that from his (God's) glorious, unlimited resources he will empower you (person's name) with inner strength through his Spirit. Then Christ will make his home in your hearts as you trust in him. Your roots will grow down into God's love and keep you strong. And may you have the power to understand, as all God's people should, how wide, how long, how high, and how deep his love is. May you experience the love of Christ, though it is too great to understand fully. Then you will be made complete with all the fullness of life and power that comes from God" (Ephesians 3:16-19, NLT, parenthetical indications mine).

Chapter Eighteen

HOPE FOR YOUR FUTURE

"'For I know the plans I have for you' declares the Lord, 'plans to prosper you and not to harm you, plans to give you a hope and a future'."
~ *Jeremiah 29:11 (NIV)*

(This is one of my favorite promises of God and a verse I'll refer to often in this chapter.)

Wednesdays are my favorite day of the week. They are my regularly scheduled lunch date with my daughter at school. I usually take her lunch and stay for recess and music class. It's the only day of the week she tells me she loves me without me telling her I love her first. For this reason, I know she really appreciates my efforts to spend a special day with her each week.

After weeks and weeks of taking her dumplings from Cracker Barrel, she decided she wanted to change things up and get 4 crunchy, beef tacos—with lettuce only—from Taco Bell. I usually bring my own sandwich for lunch, as I am lactose intolerant and the dumplings don't sit well with me. But, tacos—with no cheese—are right down my alley.

On the particular day she requested Taco Bell, I had a parent/teacher conference scheduled during her recess, but joined her afterwards for music class. In music, they are currently practicing for their upcoming Christmas production. The teacher announced she would be doing auditions for a nativity scene during their Christmas festivities. There are only two available slots for girls, and at least ten girls who want to play Mary, including my daughter. For the tryouts, each person was given the assignment to practice the chorus from the song "Reckless Love" by Cory Asbury.

When I heard this and knew there was only one Mary and at least ten girls who wanted the part, I had a flashback to the conference with my daughter's teacher. The teacher indicated my daughter is very smart, but has little confidence in herself. And, it's true. She has a very poor self-image, which I try to boost with words of affirmation as often as I can.

Realizing my daughter had a one-in-ten chance, I contacted her mother, told her about the auditions, and indicated they should start practicing. My daughter loves to sing, and I knew getting the part would provide a boost in her spirit. As I write this, I am praying for her to do her best, for God to give her the opportunity to shine for Him, and for her to have a positive attitude, regardless of the outcome.

I pray for my daughter every day. I pray the same prayers over her each day, persistently seeking God's presence in her life. One of the things I pray for her is this:

> "Father, I pray my daughter will feel Your love for her, and my love for her, deep within her soul today. I pray she

is able to shun all negativity and that You will replace any lies from the devil with joy and peace in her spirit."

I want to take you back to that day in music class, to a place where the negative lies of the devil consumed my daughter's conscious. The kids were practicing the entirety of "Reckless Love" for the production. If you've never heard the song, look it up. The song speaks of how great God's love is for us, the extent to which He'll go to fight for us, and is a powerful narrative of His unfailing love.

I knew the song from listening to K-Love Radio on a daily basis and sang along with the class. In fact, I didn't just sing, I worshipped God for loving me so deeply. I even raised my hands in Surrendered worship a few times—which translated into a few strange looks from my daughter's classmates. Though she goes to a Christian school, not all of the kids who attend are growing up in Christian homes, many of them never having witnessed genuine worship.

My daughter has a very sweet and tender spirit. As she noticed the looks and a few snickers, she began to weep with crocodile tears. I took her outside the class and asked what was wrong. She said she was upset because the other children were making fun of me. I just smiled and told her there was nothing to be ashamed or upset about.

I then told her the story of when King David returned to Jerusalem with the Ark of the Covenant (ever seen *Raiders of the Lost Ark?*), which had formerly been stolen by enemies of God and foes of His people, Israel. The story, as found in 2 Samuel 6, says that the King danced, uninhibited, before God to celebrate the victory and the return of the Ark. The story also accounts how David was ridiculed for His *embarrassing* mannerisms. His response was that it didn't matter what others thought. He wasn't dancing for them, but for God! I told my precious daughter that it didn't matter what other people thought and that *we* knew God was worthy of all our praise. She smiled and returned to class.

An Imperfect World

We live in a world that is so much different from the perfect environment God originally created. The imperfect—even fallen—state in which we live is a direct result of our selfish, Independent, and Rebellious nature. We are told, however, that one day things will be restored to a perfected realm of existence (see Revelation 21:1-4). On that day, things on earth will be as they are—currently—in heaven.

As Jesus taught His disciples to pray, He assured them (and us) that we have a loving Father in heaven and encouraged us to always give God the worship and respect He deserves—"Our Father in heaven, hollowed be your name" (see Matthew 6:9, NIV). Immediately following how we should address our heavenly Father, Jesus says we are to pray, let "Your kingdom come, your will be done, on earth as it is in heaven" (Matthew 6:10, NIV).

I know that in heaven, once all judgement has been made, those who have Trusted Jesus as their Savior will be ushered into a new heaven and a new earth. A place where there will be no more tears, death, sorrow, crying or pain (see Revelation 21:4). All who have placed their faith in Jesus can find confidence in the *hopeful future of heaven*. No more worries about finances. No distress over disease or disabilities. No more crying yourself to sleep, struggling with depression, anxiety, or any other emotional imparity.

Since that is the way things will be for us *in the future* and the way things are *now* in heaven, I often pray things here on earth will be as they are in heaven—just as Jesus directed us to do. I pray God will wipe away my daughter's tears and give her courage because she knows He is with her and for her. I pray for people who are sick, believing there is no sickness in heaven and asking God to remove individual sickness here on earth. I pray for my nieces to discover God's perfect plan for their lives and to have the courage and strength to follow through. I pray for my mom—who always has way too much on her plate—to find strength and endurance, but also for her to be filled with joy and peace. I pray that my actions will reflect my heavenly Father and draw people to His love and into His Kingdom.

I believe the hope and future God promises us in Jeremiah 29:11 is something most people reject as a realm of possibility, let alone reality. For this reason we pray timid prayers for freedom from our fears or struggles. These are great prayers, but freedom from anxiety is asking for too little. It's not heaven on earth. Instead we should ask God to free us to be able to excel, succeed, and make a difference for His Kingdom in the lives of our families, friends, coworkers, and even the world. We seem to have a sense that a *hopeful future* includes a life without troubles, trials, or discouragement. Trials are what enable us to reflect the love of God to others and remind the people we love that God always comes through.

> "Blessed [gratefully praised and adored] be the God and Father of our Lord Jesus Christ, the Father of mercies and the God of all comfort, who comforts and encourages us in every trouble so that we will be able to comfort and encourage those who are in any kind of trouble, with the comfort with which we ourselves are comforted by God. For just as Christ's sufferings are ours in abundance [as they overflow to His followers], so also our comfort [our reassurance, our encouragement, our consolation] is abundant through Christ [it is truly more than enough to endure what we must]. But if we are troubled and distressed, it is for your comfort

and salvation; or if we are comforted and encouraged, it is for your comfort, which works [in you] when you patiently endure the same sufferings which we experience. And our hope for you [our confident expectation of good for you] is firmly grounded [assured and unshaken], since we know that just as you share as partners in our sufferings, so also you share as partners in our comfort" (2 Corinthians 1:3-7, AMP).

A life of ease is not the reality of the current state of our world. That's not what this chapter is about. A hopeful future doesn't mean a new car, home, winning the lottery, or gleaning the latest technological device. It doesn't mean a life without indecision or mindful infiltration by the enemy of our souls—the devil.

Hopeful expectation for your future means Trusting God in the midst of discomfort and truly believing He is for us, not against us. I can't promise you a life without trials, temptations, or days where nothing happens without a downward spiral included. Instead, God promises to comfort you in the midst of trying times and enables you to share the hopeful future you're currently living with others.

Too many of us want ease more than comfort. God offers our souls comfort in every situation. That may include an ease in our trials—if we pay enough attention to notice. But, God never promises us an "easy street" lifestyle. If that were the case, Jesus would have taken the easy way out and called down fire on His enemies instead of dying for them.

Jesus tells us in John 16:33 that here in this fallen and imperfect world we will have "many trials and sorrows." But He also reassures us by saying, "But take heart, because I have overcome the word" (NLT). Taking heart and Trusting God is the essence of living in His *Sweet Spot*. Despite our circumstances, believing God will see us through even the most difficult times is where genuine *hope for our future* is birthed and exists.

The song, "Because He Lives,"[23] by Bill and Gloria Gaither, is one of the songs my mom wants sung at her funeral. At her prompting, I added the chorus of this inspiring hymn to this section of the book. The chorus of the song is the epitome of living in a world that is full of disappointment, yet Trusting God for a hopeful future:

> "Because he lives,
> I can face tomorrow.
> Because he lives,
> All fear is gone;
> Because I know
> He holds the future.
> And life is worth the living,
> Just because he lives."

As I read through the New Testament and study the prominent prayers of people like the Apostle Paul, I can't find any reference in His prayers to living a life of ease. Instead, I read prayers for God's people to grow in love, in wisdom and understanding, and to live with an upright character (see Philippians 1:9-11). Prayers are offered for followers of God to be strengthened by the power of the Holy Spirit (see Ephesians 3:16). Paul doesn't pray for people to have bigger homes, better jobs, more money, or to escape adversity in order to have a sense of hopefulness in their future. Instead, he prays for others to have endurance, patience, and joy—even in the midst of trials (see Colossians 1:11). As we seek hope for our future, our complete Trust in the unfailing, immeasurable love of God is our only pathway to fullness of life and for experiencing the power of God at work in our circumstances (see Ephesians 3:18-19).

The prayers of Paul are all prayers we should be praying for ourselves and for others if we are to fully realize the *hope and future* God has in store for each and every one of us. In addition to praying for us to grow in love, wisdom, patient endurance, joy in every circumstance, and the power of God's Spirit to stand up under any challenge with Godly character, the Apostle Paul offers us an example of prayer that encompasses all of these things and comes with the promise of the *hopeful future* we all desire to be our own:

> "...*We ask God to give you complete knowledge of his will* and to give you spiritual wisdom and understanding. Then the way you live will always honor and please the Lord, and *your lives will produce every kind of good fruit*. All the while, *you will grow as you learn to know God better and better*" (Colossians 1:9-10, NLT, emphases mine).

How, then, do we know if we're living a Kingdom lifestyle or following God's perfect will for our lives? How can we be certain? How can we be sure we're living the kind of Kingdom life we're instructed to pray toward? *The answer is in knowing God better.*

Knowing, Trusting, Loving, And Finding Contentment

I'm sure you've noticed by now the theme of prayer—especially praying God's Word over our circumstances—to be prevalent throughout our journey toward, our desire to live inside of, and the choices we make to stay in *God's Sweet Spot*. It will be through your Surrendered heart, conscious actions, meditation on God's Word, and diligent prayer that you move *from the frustration of running-on-empty to the fulfillment of life overflowing*. These same disciplines will also move you closer to understanding God's perfect plan for your life and help you find hope for your future.

When Jesus was teaching His disciples—and us—to pray (*The Lord's Prayer*), He continues His teaching by freeing us to ask things of God on our behalf. He demonstrates this by saying, "Give us today our daily bread" (see Matthew 9:11, NIV). When I dissect Jesus' prayer and get to "give us," I immediately think of provisions.

I have to confess I've been a bit anxious about my finances since quitting my job to write this book. The devil puts all kinds of "what if" questions in my head. As such, I've been running around—sometimes eleven hours a day—delivering food because I felt like I needed the money.

Just recently, I got on my knees and prayed. I confessed my fears about my future to God and asked Him to help me. I asked if I was to continue delivering or if He was going to provide a job for me other than driving. The answer I got wasn't one I expected.

After praying, eating some dinner, and relaxing a bit on the couch, I got up to ready myself for bed. It was then I had an overwhelming sense that I was not to worry any more. Nor was I to take things into my own hands by exhausting myself through the delivery service.

God had asked me to quit my job so I could write. I always came home from my former job wiped out. I rarely had any energy to write. The same thing was happening with the delivery service. After eleven hours on the road, I had no energy to write. God prompted my spirit to let me know He would provide my *daily bread*; I simply needed to provide spiritual nourishment to those who desperately need to embrace the concepts of the book He'd instructed me to write.

You may be in a position right now where you genuinely have need of *bread*. Or, perhaps you need a job. Maybe the environment of your current job necessitates a new and better job. Realizing there's a difference between essential needs and desired wants, Jesus tells us it's okay to ask God for our needs. In fact, not only is it *okay*, but according to Jesus' demonstrated prayer, we *should* ask for what we need.

If we dig a little deeper and consider other daily provisions we need, we find the Bible says, *"...People do not live by bread alone, but by every word that comes from the mouth of God"* (Matthew 4:4, NLT). This is the answer to finding our purpose in life. Our daily provision is not just food, clothing, shelter, a job, or any other material thing. I believe that's why Jesus arranged His teaching on prayer in the way He did. He basically tells us to ask God to show us the way we should live—here on earth—and then tells us that we'll need some provisions along the way. I'm interpreting what Jesus says; but, I believe the bread (provision) we need most is the Bread of life—God's Word.

Read, Read, Read

In addition to my daily prayers for my daughter's emotional life, I also pray for her spiritual life and God's ultimate purposes for her. I've been praying this same prayer for my daughter since before she was even born:

> "Father, I ask you to help my daughter know You, trust You, love You, and find contentment in You alone—all the days of her life. And, I pray she leads others to do the same."

After years of praying that prayer for my daughter, I realized I needed to be praying that same prayer for myself too. If I want to find the kind of hope for my future Jeremiah 29:11 speaks of, the first thing I need to do is get to know God better.

Only by getting to know God better will I learn to Trust Him more. By Trusting Him more, the result will be a deeper love for Him. Out of my Trusting love for God, contentment will manifest itself in every situation in life. And, as a culmination of all of this, I will be living my purpose of a life that is pleasing to God and that is attractive to others. In this way, God's Kingdom will come as people are drawn into His love and grace by learning to know Him, Trust Him, love Him, and find contentment in Him, alone.

Stop! Slow down; and, reread the previous paragraph again, dissecting it and discerning the best nuggets of wisdom you'll ever gain. Knowing comes before Trust. Trust is followed by love. Knowing, Trusting and loving all result in contentment. That's what we're after, isn't it? Isn't the culmination of knowing, Trusting, loving, and finding contentment the definition of *God's Sweet Spot*?

So far, we've been stuck in a cycle of Complacency, Frustration, Independence, Rebellion, and Trouble. And, I've encouraged you with action-points along the way to cut your cycle short and discover the sugary peace of Trusting in God and living in His *Sweet Spot*. As we journey forward, we want to replace our old cyclical actions—that only dig us deeper and deeper into a rut—with the kind of mountaintop experience that can only be found in developing a new cycle of knowing God, Trusting Him, loving Him with all of our hearts, finding contentment in Him alone, and sharing our joy with others. *This is your purpose in life. This is your hope for the future.*

Regardless of whether you feel a special need to be a godly and loving parent, an example in your workplace of God's love, to start a Bible study for single mom's, invest—out of your abundance—in God's kingdom through what others are doing, become a missionary, a pastor, a songwriter, or whatever passion God has put in your heart, your first and most important purpose in life is to *start by getting to know God better*. Only then will the rest come to full fruition.

If you could precisely describe the events that would need to take place in order for you to feel like you have hope for your future, what would each step of the transformation look like? Maybe you want to marry a Godly person, raise a family who will know, Trust, and love God, finding contentment in Him all the days of their lives. How does that transpire? Perhaps you desire a job that will provide for your needs, with enough left over to give generously to those in need. Maybe you want to be a better reflection of God's love in the workplace. What steps do you need to take to see your dreams become a reality? Will your best laid plans be fully dependent on God's direction or your own Independent speculation and planning?

For me, I want this book to be published, attract the attention of churches, Christian counseling centers, recovery hubs, and people who are desperate for change regardless of their Troubles. Ultimately, I want this book to go viral, become a *New York Times* Bestseller, and change hundreds of thousands of lives. Of course, the esteem of being a best-selling author and the income these things would provide are enticing, but knowing lives are being changed is more valuable than admiration or wealth. In fact, my singular desire is for this book to lead just one person (maybe you) into an intimate fellowship with God and change your life forever. That being the case, just one life transformed will be worth all my efforts. So, how do I accomplish my dream?

If I follow the marketing gurus' advice, the independent publishing house's direction, hire a professional editor, and stumble upon a large sum of money to pay for it all, my expectations for this book will come together like a well-oiled machine. Or so I'm told.

It's been on my mind lately to use my extensive credit line to charge the $15,000 I know will bring instant success for my writing efforts. Coaching, press releases, television and radio interviews, social media campaigns, banner ads, catalog advertising, eBook formatting, commendable royalties, custom design for my cover, and internal formatting are all a part of the deal. I could basically leave God out of the equation, go into debt, and make a real go of things.

I know, however, going into debt is not God's plan for me or for this book. I want to live inside *God's Sweet Spot* by living out *His* hope-filled plans for my future (see Jeremiah 29:11) instead of doing things *my*, Independent from God, way. As such, if I truly want to see the concepts of this book change lives, going into debt isn't the investment I need to make. Instead, the first thing I need to invest in is getting to know God better.

Getting to know God leads to Trust, love and contentment. This kind of investment will produce far more than the plans I have for myself. When I know God better, my Trust will increase. As my Trust increases, I won't worry about how to get the words God has given me distributed to the masses. Instead, I'll trust Him to get His words to those who need them most.

Getting to know God and allowing my Trust in and love for Him to grow will take time and intentionality. There's no magic wand or promise of instant gratification. Just like any other relationship we choose to build, our relationship with God will require an investment if we want to see it flourish into the kind of Kingdom and purposeful life God desires for us.

> "...Do not be conformed to this world [any longer with its superficial values and customs], but be transformed and progressively changed [as you mature spiritually] by the renewing of your mind [focusing on godly values

and ethical attitudes], so that you may prove [for yourselves] what the will of God is, that which is good and acceptable and perfect [in His plan and purpose for you]" (Romans 12:2, AMP).

The best way to be progressively transformed in your spiritual life, renew your mind, and discover God's best laid plan for your life is to get to know God by spending time with Him, reading His written Word, and by praying about what you learn. Out of this intimate time with God, your deepest purpose in life will be made clear and *hope for your future will become a reality*.

Many people, however, believe there's just not enough time in the day to sit down and read the Bible. To this I respond by saying, "You will never have enough time in your day to accomplish the things that *really matter* if you don't spend time in God's Word." The Bible is God's instruction manual for life. It teaches us what our priorities should be, where to expend our limited time, and shows us the best possible way to live.

> "All Scripture is God-breathed [given by divine inspiration] and is profitable for instruction, for conviction [of sin], for correction [of error and restoration to obedience], for training in righteousness [learning to live in conformity to God's will, both publicly and privately—behaving honorably with personal integrity and moral courage]" (2 Timothy 3:16, AMP).

If you want to know how to live—especially as it relates to God's perfect will for your life—you must *read, read, read*. I keep a Bible in every room of my house, except for the bathroom and kitchen. I don't keep a Bible in the kitchen because I make a mess when I cook. I don't keep a Bible in the bathroom because I always take my phone with me to the bathroom and I have a Bible app on my phone. I even keep a Bible in my car. This way, I have no excuse for not reading.

At multiple points during my busy day, I *always* have at least a few moments for reflection. You do too! It's just a matter of whether you decide to reflect on the many outlets of negativity in this world or on the positive Truths that can transform your entire life for the better. I choose the positive and always have a Bible within life-changing reach.

I understand reading the Bible may seem like a *drastic measure*, but I'm going to show you how to take *baby steps* into creating a multifaceted devotional life, which includes reading God's Word. Eventually, your baby steps will lead you to intentional—even sporadic—moments of tuning into what God has to say. You'll soon discover a craving for God's Word, His *implicit* instructions, and *focused* indications for specific areas of your life. You'll find the Bible to be the greatest resource you've ever known, if you simply choose to *read, read, read*.

Consider just a few thoughts—though there are many—from *one* single chapter of Scripture that encourage us to make spending intentional time in God's Word a priority. This committed time will be profitable for our souls and ensure *hopeful expectation* in our daily encounters with life circumstances:

> "I seek you with all my heart; do not let me stray from your commands. I have hidden your word in my heart that I might not sin against you" (Psalm 119:10-11, NIV).

> "With all my heart I want your blessings. Be merciful as you promised. I pondered the direction of my life, and I turned to follow your laws" (Psalm 119:58-59, NLT).

"Before I was afflicted I went astray, but now I obey your word. You are good, and what you do is good; teach me your decrees" (Psalm 119:66-67, NIV).

"My soul faints with longing for your salvation, but I have put my hope in your word" (Psalm 119:81, NIV).

"How sweet are your words to my taste, sweeter than honey to my mouth!" (Psalm 119:103, NIV).

"Your word is a lamp to guide my feet and a light for my path" (Psalm 119:105, NLT).

"Your laws are my treasure; they are my heart's delight. I am determined to keep your decrees to the very end" (Psalm 119:111-112, NLT).

"The teaching of your word gives light, so even the simple can understand. I pant with expectation, longing for your commands" (Psalm 119:130-131, NLT).

"I rise before dawn and cry for help; I have put my hope in your word" (Psalm 119:147, NIV).

❖ ***Reading Made Easy***

As you begin taking *baby steps* toward discovering the benefits of spending time reading God's Word, my first suggestion is to find a translation of the Bible that is easy for you to understand (as mentioned before). The New Living Translation (NLT) and the New International Version (NIV) are easier to read than many traditional translations, as they utilize a vernacular many of us are used to hearing and speaking.

If you want to embrace a deeper understanding—without having to refer to other people's interpretations—the Amplified Bible (AMP) is a great resource. There are also Biblical compilations of several translations compared side-by-side. These are known as "parallel" Bibles.

If, however, you are struggling financially and a new purchase is out of reach right now, the internet is a great place to find everything you need. Biblegateway.com is a great online resource and Bible.com provides a multi-version app for all of your digital devices.

Once you've armed yourself with a personalized translation of choice, find a thick stack of index cards, a new composition book, and a pen. Each of these items will prove valuable as you seek to know God more intimately and discern God's best laid plans, which are your only hope for a fulfilling future.

When it comes to what to read, the entire Bible is filled with the knowledge of who God is, His purposes for our lives, and the consequences for doing things our own—Independent—ways. As we consider *baby steps* in getting to know God, I have a few suggestions on what and how to read—for maximized benefit.

❖ **Where To Start**

My current reading schedule includes a chapter from the New Testament Book of James each day. It's only five chapters long, so I simply start over every five days. Additionally, I read a chapter a day from the Old Testament Book of Proverbs. I switch this up occasionally, but always try to read something from the New and Old Testaments each day.

As you get started—especially if this is your first *real* attempt at making Bible reading a part of your daily routine—I'd suggest starting with the Gospel of John. This New Testament account of Jesus' life, teachings, death, and resurrection is the one Gospel (out of four: Matthew, Mark Luke, and John) which clearly depicts Jesus as being God in fleshly form. Though you'll see a lot of the stories repeated in the four Gospel accounts—from a slightly varying perspective—I'd also suggest the Gospel of Matthew, as it includes a hefty portion of Jesus' practical teachings.

Each of the Gospels tells similar stories and account similar teachings. The difference between the four is that each is written from a different perspective. I compare it to four people witnessing an automobile accident. Each person saw the same things, but describes the happenings according to their own personality and perspective.

Each Gospel also provides a narrative that is particular to the audience to whom the author is writing (which is important). If the writer is to a Greek audience, the references will be identifiable. If, however, the reader is Hebrew or Jewish in character, the description might differ. The story is the same; the illustrative narrative might, however, differ.

One of the most practical compilations of instructions on living life according to God's plan is the New Testament letter, written by James. I find so many nuggets for living in *God's Sweet Spot* in the Book of James that I read and refer to it often. Another practical book of wisdom is the Book of Proverbs. There are 31 chapters in Proverbs, which makes it easy to read one chapter per day for each day of the month. And, you'll never lose your place, because all you have to do is look at your calendar to see what chapter you should be reading.

Once you've read John, James, Matthew, and Proverbs, I'd suggest reading the entire New Testament. The easiest way to do this is to read a whole chapter—or even a section of a chapter—each day, combined with a chapter in Proverbs. This may seem like a lot to chew on at a time. That's why I often suggest reading from section to section within a chapter, as most translations have subdivided headings within each chapter. I promise you that God is not keeping up with how many chapters you read. Instead, He's more interested in the dedicated time you spend with Him.

Also, as you read, use your notecards to write down specific verses or passages that spawn thoughts or engage your mindset. I have a whole stack of notecards I refer to often when praying for specific needs or situations. If you take this exercise of writing notecards seriously, I'm guessing you'll fill half a deck with the practical inspirations you'll find in James and in Proverbs.

Reading, copying—even memorizing—certain Scriptures, and utilizing them in your prayer life will encourage your heart, deepen your understanding of God, and *move you closer to a future filled with hope*. These hand-written notecards will also prove useful when encouraging others who desperately need God's hope, inspiration, and direction in their own life circumstances. So, keep your stack of notecards with you at all times. The best way to keep them all together is to bind them with a rubber band or purchase one of those packs that are already spirally bound.

❖ ***Knowing God By Getting The Most Out Of What You Read***

I get the most out of reading when I write notecards pertaining to things I need to know and remember about God, His love, and His instructions for life. Another practice which helps me stay focused and truly sense God's heart for me is to journal in a composition book about my reading for the day. Here are some simple instructions to get you started in a discipline which will prove invaluable to you—each day—and allow you to reflect on God's goodness, faithfulness, and specific direction for your life:

1) Obtain a new composition book;

2) On the first page you may want to write a note to yourself concerning why you're choosing to make God's Word a priority, or simply use this page as a title page for your journaling;

3) Flip the first page so you have two full pages facing you. The full two pages are available for your use, specific to the passage or chapter you'll be reading. Keeping everything together and accessible within a two-page summary will help you as you reflect back on your reading;

4) At the top of the page, write the date on which you are reading and the reference for the chapter or passage you'll be reading;

5) Before reading, pray. Ask God for wisdom and direction. I would suggest praying the following—even writing the prayer just beneath the day's date and scripture reference:

"Father, I pray for wisdom as I read. Reveal Yourself to me. Help me to know You better through this time of reading and meditating on Your Word. Instruct me in ways that allow me to both grow in my faith and in my actions. In Jesus' name; amen."

6) Read your selected passage(s) or chapter(s);

7) As you read, make notes—including particular verse references—concerning those things in which God is instructing or reassuring you. NOTE: You may feel, at times, as though a particular verse applies to someone else. If the verse will encourage that person, please share your thoughts—with humility—never making digs at others with verses you deem applicable to his/her Independent or Rebellious state;

8) Also make notes concerning things you read but aren't sure about their intended meaning. This will allow you to do some further research or seek counsel in adding definition to your reading;

9) After reading, use the rest of the space you have available on the two allotted pages to write a prayer to God. Ask Him to clarify things that are unclear. Ask Him to help you apply what you've learned. Also thank Him for the time to get to know Him better and for His best laid plans you're your life.

To give you a clear example of getting to know God better by reading and meditating on His Word—so you can further Trust Him, love Him, and find contentment in His hopeful plan for your future—the following is an example of how I would treat James 1:1-27:

James 1:1-27   Today's Date

> *"Father, I pray for wisdom as I read. Reveal Yourself to me. Help me to know You better through this time of reading and meditating on Your Word. Instruct me in ways that allow me to grow both my faith and in my actions. In Jesus' name; amen."*

Vs. 2-4   It is inevitable that I will face trials in life; how I respond to them is up to me. My response will allow me to gauge the level of my growth in knowing and Trusting God.

Vs. 5-8   God wants to give me His wisdom, helping me discern my daily path and His best choices for me along the way. When He gives me clarity in a particular area, I should not doubt His promptings, but consider them to be tangible Truths. This will require me to take courageous and active steps, according to His direction.

Vs. 13-15   I am always faced with a choice when I feel tempted to operate outside of God's best. I cannot blame my inconsistencies on anyone—including the devil. I am responsible for resisting my own sinful desires.

V. 17   Every good thing I have is a gift from God. I may have played a part—through my actions—in receiving a blessing; but, without God's grace, any accolade would be futile and fleeting.

Vs. 19-20   I need to listen more than I talk. No matter how entitled I may feel to lash out at a person who angers me, my actions will not reflect the kind of grace I expect God to show me when I am in the wrong.

Vs. 22-25   When God shows me something in His word that will help me and others, I need to act on what I've read and learned. Otherwise, I'm treating God's Word as something I glance through instead of the power by which I live, breathe, and find purpose.

Vs. 26-27   I need to keep a tight rein on my tongue, help others who are in need, and keep my distance from anything or anyone who might cause me to be led astray from God's absolute best for my life.

Prayer:

"Father, I am not the most patient person. I don't like being in the midst of trying circumstances. Help me to be more patient and enduring when trials come my way. I want to grow in confident hope and react toward others the way You would react. Help me to control my tongue and my anger. Help me to listen more than

I speak. Give me the wisdom to interact with everyday circumstances and the discernment to make wise decisions in the things that matter most. I am often a very selfish person, Lord. Help me to consider others and help those who are most in need. Help me, Lord, to do more than read. I want to selflessly act on what I read. I want to know You and reflect your love and grace to the world around me. In Jesus' name; amen."

Knowing God intimately is the best place to start if you truly desire hope for your future. Reading His Word, following His direction, and keeping record of your thoughts will keep you centered and growing in Trust, Love, and Contentment as each relates to your relationship with God and to your future.

Selah (Pause for Reflection)

Take *15 Minutes* and Make this Chapter *Personal*

> *NOTE: Always keep a Bible, notebook, and pen ready.*
> ***Why?*** *I believe God will open himself up to you during this time of reflection, just as He does for me.*

As you consider the hope that is your future, it's important to embrace the Truths of God's Word. For example, you can know that God is for you—even working overtime to see things turn out for your absolute best (see Romans 8:28). He has broken the power of sin and death over your life. You are no longer a slave to your impulses and sin (Romans 6:13-14 and Romans 8:1-4). Instead, you have the power of God working in you to overcome even the greatest obstacles (Romans 8:31-39).

I just listed three vital promises—made directly to you—all from *one* chapter of the Bible. And there are many more. These are the kinds of things you will learn to become more and more confident in as you read God's Word, take it to heart, and put it into action in everything you do. As you get to know God through His Word, you will be able to make definitive statements like the ones above, and claim the victory of a hopeful life through **Daily Declarations** like the ones listed below:

1) I am a new creature in Christ, forgiven and free of shame and condemnation, washed by His powerful blood (2 Corinthians 5:17, Romans 8:1);

2) I live by faith, not by sight or by feelings, and my faith is rooted in the eternal Word of God (2 Corinthians 5:7, 2 Corinthians 2:6-7);

3) I refuse to receive a spirit of fear today because I am given by God a spirit of power, love, and self-control (2 Timothy 1:7);

4) I can do all things today through Christ as He gives me strength. His strength is made perfect in my weaknesses, and whatever I face today, He will give me the strength to match it and to overcome it (Philippians 4:13, 2 Corinthians 12:9, 10);

5) I am fearfully and wonderfully made by God. I am His workmanship, His masterpiece. Therefore, I will praise Him at all times, and I will not walk in insecurity (Psalm 139:14, Ephesians 2:10);

6) As I am obedient in the areas of tithing and giving, God will supply all of my needs, He will give me power to gain wealth and add no trouble to it, will increase my store of seed, and will cause me to live in crazy favor (Philippians 4:19, Malachi 3:10, 11, 2 Corinthians 9:10, 11);

7) I am blessed to be a blessing. I will sow and reap generously on every occasion, will live to give cheerfully, and will learn to steward well God's blessings in my life (2 Corinthians 9:6, 7, 11, Matthew 25:21);

8) I have everything I need today concerning life and godliness. Therefore, I will live a pure life, striving for the holiness of God, casting down vain imaginations, taking disobedient thoughts captive, and walking in my identity in Christ (2 Peter 1:3,4, 2 Corinthians 10:5,6);

9) My home is built on Christ and will stand when the storms hit. My children are blessed and protected, and as for me and my household, we will serve the Lord (Matthew 7:24-25, Proverbs 10:25, Prov. 14:26, Joshua 24:15);

10) Today I will increase in favor with God and man, in compassion for others, in anointing and godly influence, in wisdom, and in faith (2 Peter 1:5-7).

These are called *Daily Declarations* for a reason. They are confident promises of God you can begin claiming over your life and your family's lives on a day-to-day basis. Please take the time to look up the Bible references and know God has a *hopeful future* in store for you.

Daily Declarations written by Founding Pastor, Jay Stewart,
The Refuge Church, Kannapolis, NC, www.TheRefuge.net (Used with permission).[24]

Chapter Nineteen

FORGIVE(N)ESS

"Every grievance you hold hides a little more of the light of the world from your eyes until the darkness becomes overwhelming. Everything you forgive restores that light. So ask yourself, who is it that you are really hurting?"
~ Donna Goddard, author of the Waldmeer Series[25]

How much time do you spend driving each day? Consider your daily commute to and from work, picking the kids up from school, soccer or band practice, a trip to the grocery store, the pharmacy, or wherever life takes you. Many of us spend hours in our cars each and every day.

For some, however, you may not drive at all. In many greater metropolitan areas, it's easier to take the train, bus, ride your bike, or simply walk to work. Owning a car, paying for parking, and the hassles of urban driving are often more of a liability than an asset. In fact, a current trend among Millennials is to live close to work and utilize alternative transportation for everyday living—including using services like Lyft or Uber—because it's less expensive than insurance premiums, having a car payment, and the rising costs of gasoline.

Whether you drive, take the bus, train, ride your bike, or use some other form of transportation, we all have a commute. We all have places to go, things to do, and people to see. And, no matter your mode of transport, I'm guessing we all have frustrations when it comes to getting where we're going.

For me, I have a strong distaste for driving. It's in my car where I get the most aggravated, say and think the worst things about people, and find myself asking for God's forgiveness at least a dozen times a day because my attitude doesn't reflect His love.

I have, however, recently begun doing my best to practice the *Golden Rule* while driving: *"Do to others what you would have them do to you"* (see Matthew 7:12, NIV). If I realize the person behind me wants to go faster than I'm currently driving, I either speed up or get out of the way. When I'm unsure of my destination or next turn, I'll often forego driving incredibly slow as I look for an address or slamming on brakes to make the on-point turn. I'd rather pass my turn, find a safe place to turn around, and go back to my missed opportunity than inconvenience the person behind me. Additionally, I often let people out in front of me in traffic and even semi-brake for crazy squirrels.

Even with all of those practices in place, I still have momentary lapses of reason. For example, if you pull out in front of me on a busy two-lane road and immediately put on your left turn signal, my eyes glow red, shoot imaginary bolts of lightning through your back window, and my hands go up in a tirade that resembles a seizure.

Yes; I have issues! But so do you. Too many of us are quick to judge others based on driving habits, race, economic status, level of education, political affiliation, their clothes, how those clothes are worn, or even the music they listen to.

Jesus said, "*Do not judge, or you too will be judged. For in the same way you judge others, you will be judged, and with the measure you use, it will be measured to you*" (Matthew 7:1-2, NIV). Yet, my eyes still dart and my arms often flail because of *the exact same driving concerns I display on a regular basis*. In fact, I catch myself—almost daily—fussing about someone's driving, then realizing I pulled the exact same move yesterday, today, or even a minute ago.

A friend of mine told me of a road-rage situation he'd been a part of that now makes me think twice before judging another person's current driving pattern. He'd been behind a car whose driver seemed unaware she was holding up traffic, with a long line of cars backed up behind her. Much like me, he ranted, raved, and used a little sign language to reflect his frustration. When he finally had the opportunity to pass the seemingly oblivious driver, he looked over at her with that kind of peering stare that's supposed to—somehow—change things. When he looked her way, however, he noticed she was uncontrollably weeping.

My friend told me he felt like such a jerk. That woman may have just lost a loved one or received the most frightening or disconcerting news of her life. And, all he could think about was getting where he needed to be, faster.

Though I still struggle to keep it together behind the wheel, I pray every day—before I even crank my car. I pray that I will have a good attitude while driving, that I will keep my tongue in check, and that I will reflect the love of God to others in my driving. Maybe that person in front of me *really is* a poor driver. *Or*, perhaps, I'm just *intolerant* and view my needs to be more important than the struggle the person I'm sharing the road with may be going through.

"Do nothing out of selfish ambition or vain conceit. Rather, in humility value others above yourselves, *not looking to your own interests* but each of you to the interests of the others" (Philippians 2:3-4, NIV, *emphasis mine*).

Whether it's the distracted driver in front of you, the person in the express checkout who has three carts of groceries, or the neighbor's cat who keeps destroying your flower bed, do any of these things matter in the realm of God's Kingdom or in eternity? Perhaps, to keep yourself from such aggravating predicaments, you could leave a little earlier to get where you're going, plan your day to include a longer line at the checkout, or strategically place some cat food in another part of your yard that will attract the *infiltrator* to your compost pile instead of your flower garden. Yet it often seems to be the little things—causing us to judge, and therefore be judged—that poison our souls as much as holding a grudge or resentment against someone who's truly offended us.

Perhaps you've never considered a quick judgement of someone reflective of an unforgiving heart. If you haven't, this is a moment for true, introspective reflection. Why? Because my quick-tempered judgement reflects more about me than it does the person I believe is in the wrong (reread that last statement).

You don't have to hold a long-standing grudge or feel a particular righteous indignation toward another person to be deeply rooted in bitterness or resentment. In fact, the most common form of an unforgiving heart is often rooted in our own inability to forgive ourselves. Yes; ourselves. I know, because for years I indulged myself in the unforgiving poison of not being able to let go of my own mistakes, missteps, and imprudent behavior.

No matter the root, an unforgiving, judgmental heart will leave you bitter, lonely, tired, and Frustrated. That's not the place God wants you to dwell. In fact, it's the antithesis of living a life *overflowing with hope for your future*. Choosing a life marked by forgiveness is a critical step on your journey toward experiencing a life of joy and fulfillment. So, how do we find freedom from the kinds of ruts where we misalign judgement on the unsuspecting, those who seemingly deserve our wrath, or even on ourselves?

Forgiven: It Started with God

When I walk into a grocery store, I'm always armed with a shopping list. I already know what I need and I've usually calculated what I'm going to spend before walking through the doors.

Right now my grocery list is fairly short. I need deodorant, would like to pick up some flavored water additives, popcorn kernels, coconut oil, pickled jalapeño peppers, hotdog buns, frozen french fries, some slightly green bananas, shredded cabbage, and a large onion.

Just like you, however, I'm always tempted to pick up a little something extra, especially if I'm hungry when I get to the store. But, since I'm trying to keep from spending anything extra on my credit cards, I use cash. As such, I keep a running tab in my head concerning how much I'm spending. Only if I know I have some breathing room will I add anything to the list.

If you, too, want to become a grocery shopping aficionado, consider the steps I take to make the most of my trip:

1) I know what's needed;
2) I count the costs and always have a plan before I start;
3) I account for detours along the way.

When it comes to being *forgiven*, I believe God's plan for forgiveness has some similarities to the way in which I approach grocery shopping. Let's take a look at how each of my shopping strategies aligns with God's plan.

❖ *What's Needed*

The harsh reality is that our Complacent, Frustrated, Independent, Rebellious nature—what the Bible calls sin—may seem fulfilling in the moment. But, it eventually leaves us feeling empty and in Trouble.

The ultimate result of all Trouble is an eternal separation from God. The Bible says that not only will our physical bodies eventually die (see Hebrews 9:27), but there is also a death that exceeds the physical realm— an eternal death that will be far worse than anything we can imagine—at least for those who have not been *forgiven* (see Revelation 20:11-15).

Death is required for our sin; it is the penalty that must be paid (see Romans 6:23). In fact, the Bible clearly states, "Without the shedding of blood *[death]*, there is no forgiveness" (Hebrews 9:22b, NLT, *[bracketed]* note mine).

All throughout the Old Testament, blood sacrifices were offered for the forgiveness of sin. The blood of goats, bulls, and lambs were all offered to God as sacrifices. But these ritual sacrifices had to be repeated time and time again, as no sacrifice was sufficient for our ongoing Rebellion.

In my humanity, my heart cries out, "Why?" "Why must there be death?" "Isn't there an easier, better way?" "I'm not a terrorist, murderer, or a pedophile. People like that deserve punishment—even death. But not me!"

When was the last time you saw an account of a child being abducted? When I hear of such news, I begin to wonder. I wonder if the child will ever see his or her parents again. Has the child been kidnapped and sold into some sort of human trafficking ring? Are they being, otherwise, abused or even been brutally murdered? I wonder what kind of creep would do such a thing? Does the kind of maniacal person who would do something like this live in my neighborhood?

I don't know about you, but when I hear of mass shootings, child abductions, or other such atrocities, I think to myself, "The person responsible for this should be (you fill in the blank)." In those moments, I stand as judge, juror, *and* executioner. Yet, as I translate James 4:11-12 into my own words, I read something like this: *"How dare you think yourself worthy of judging someone else? God is the only one worthy of setting the standard and consequent judgement."*

Just a few verses prior, James tells us that if we have broken *any* of God's rules for a just and rightful living, we are guilty. Guilty of one thing makes us just as guilty as if we were also murderers or adulterers or whatever else you deem to be punishable (see James 2:8-13). Even Jesus said that if we lust in our hearts, we are as guilty as the one who commits the actual act. He says that if we harbor anger in our hearts toward someone, the morality of our attitude is the same as killing them (see Matthew 5:21-30).

Who, then, am I to judge? Am I guiltless? Do not my attitudes and actions deserve prosecution and punishment?

> "For everyone has sinned; we all fall short of God's glorious standard" (Romans 3:23, NLT).

> "...The wages of sin is death..." (Romans 6:23a, NLT).

The good news for each and every one of us is there is a plan. This plan was set in motion way before the first creepy, crawling thing ever drudged itself across the face of the earth. It was God's plan. Forgiveness begins and ends with God. And this incredulous *plan* began with a ginormous BUT.

❖ A Costly Plan

Many of the greatest stories in the Bible begin with "BUT God." Though Romans 6:23 says the payment we owe God for our sins is death, the entirety of the verse gives us hope: "For the wages of sin is death, *BUT the free gift of GOD is eternal life* through Christ Jesus our Lord" (NLT, *EMPHASES* mine). Thank God there's always a BUT!

The *free* gift of God is eternal life—rather than eternal condemnation—through our faith in Jesus Christ. We get to spend eternity in a place that is so much greater than anything we can imagine. In fact, though in chapters twenty-one and twenty-two of Revelation we are given a glimpse of what heaven will be like, the Bible tells us in 1 Corinthians 2:9 that even the best literary description of heaven doesn't measure up: "What God has planned for people who love him is more than eyes have seen or ears have heard. *It has never even entered our minds!*" (CEV, *emphasis mine*).

Though this unfathomable gift of spending an eternity with the lover of our souls is *free* to us, it was *costly* for God. To emphasize the reality of God's costly—yet perfectly planned—sacrifice, consider the following scenario: Let's say you and your family become pregnant later in life. In due diligence (not to say it's morally correct), you decide to have some tests done do determine the future health of your unborn child. Results in hand, the doctors indicate you *must* have this child. According to their findings, the delivery of your baby will enable the medical world to inoculate the *entire* world's population from any cancer-related deaths. This is all due to the particular DNA your unborn child reserves in his or her cell structure. The greatest dilemma you have to consider is that your child will have to be sacrificed for the greater good of mankind. *Your child has to die so others can live*!

Could you? *Would you* do it? Regardless of your answer, "BUT God…"

> "*BUT GOD* showed his great love for us by sending Christ to die for us while we were still sinners. And since we have been made right in God's sight by the blood of Christ, he will certainly save us from God's condemnation. For since our friendship with God was restored by the death of his Son while we were still his enemies, we will certainly be saved through the life of his Son. So *now we can rejoice* in our wonderful new relationship with God because our Lord Jesus Christ has made us friends of God" (Romans 5:8-11, NLT, *EMPHASES* mine).

Our sins made us enemies of God. To be made friends with God again, our sins required a sacrifice that would supersede any other. Instead of the sacrifices required under the Law of the Old Testament, God chose to pay the price for our sins by offering Himself—in the fleshly form of Jesus—as the sacrifice to end all sacrifices.

> "Under the old covenant, the priest stands and ministers before the altar day after day, offering the same sacrifices again and again, which can never take away sins. But our High Priest (Jesus) offered himself to God as a single sacrifice for sins, good for all time. Then he sat down in the place of honor at God's right hand. There he waits until his enemies are humbled and made a footstool under his feet. For by that one offering he forever made perfect those who are being made holy. And the Holy Spirit also testifies that this is so. For he says, 'This is the new covenant I will make with my people on that day,' says the Lord: 'I will put my laws in their hearts, and I will write them on their minds.' Then he says, 'I will never again remember their sins and lawless deeds.' And when sins have been forgiven, there is no

need to offer any more sacrifices" (Hebrews 10:11-18, NLT, parenthetical note mine).

❖ Detours

Just like my regular trips to the grocery store, God accounts for detours. In fact, He accounted for them way before he engaged the sordid grocery-list of our lives.

> "For you know that God paid a ransom to save you from the empty life you inherited from your ancestors. And it was not paid with mere gold or silver, which lose their value. It was the precious blood of Christ, the sinless, spotless Lamb of God. *God chose him as your ransom long before the world began*, but now in these last days he has been revealed for your sake" (1 Peter 1:18-20, NLT, *emphasis mine*).

God knew what was needed. He knew we couldn't pay our bill. He paid the price for us. And, His grace gift-card *is never maxed out*!

Just as God's plan was to pay our sin-debt in full before time ever began, He also knew the detours we'd make in life even before we were ever born. He knew whether we'd choose His grace by placing our faith in Jesus and He knew the choices we'd make afterwards—the good, the bad, and the ugly.

> "O LORD, you have examined my heart and know everything about me. You know when I sit down or stand up. You know my thoughts even when I'm far away. You see me when I travel and when I rest at home. You know everything I do. You know what I am going to say even before I say it, LORD... You saw me before I was born.

> Every day of my life was recorded in your book. Every moment was laid out before a single day had passed. How precious are your thoughts about me, O God. They cannot be numbered! I can't even count them; they outnumber the grains of sand! And when I wake up, you are still with me" (Psalm 139:1-4, 16-18, NLT).

Have you ever tried to bargain with God, saying, "If you'll do *this* for me God, I'll do *that*;" or, "I'll *never* do *this* again if you'll just do *that*"? I have.

I remember when I first realized I needed some outside help to stop drinking. I also knew that most rehab facilities are at least 30-day inpatient programs. I felt like there was absolutely no way I could go 30 days without income. And, besides, what would happen to my business if I disappeared for 30, plus days? As a bargaining chip, I used to pray, "God, *if you'll just let me win the lottery*, the first thing I'll do after tithing and paying taxes will be to check myself into rehab."

I never did win the lottery. And, there are many reasons for that. One of which might have been because I probably would have had one last blowout of partying before checking myself in to get help. With the kind of partying a million dollars can buy, I probably wouldn't have lived long enough to remember my vow to seek help.

Though that seems like a plausible answer, it's not the real reason I never won the lottery. Instead, God knew me. He knew me intimately. And, He already had a plan for my decades of taking detours.

When I finally decided to commit my will to God's plan, I took almost 40 days off work, was able to maintain my bills, and got some much needed help. But that wasn't the end of God's plan. He knew I needed the spiritual boost I received at rehab, but He also knew there was *a much longer journey to take.*

It was at rehab where God convinced me to write this book. Even then, that wasn't the whole of His healing plan. He knew I needed to get this book out to the masses. To those who desperately need to be filled with hope for the future. But, God also knew I needed this book. I needed to write it. I needed to live it. I needed more than a million dollars; I needed His *perfectly laid plan* to become my *perfectly laid life*.

When the Bible says every day of my life was laid out even before it began, that doesn't mean I'm a puppet in God's hands. He didn't decide to write my life—day-by-day—into some sultry paperback or heroic novel. Instead, He already knew everything I'd ever do, every choice I'd ever make, and He made plans—hundreds and thousands of plans—to rewrite and edit the mistakes I'd make into stories that would turn out for my good. Romans 8:28 says *"And we know [with great confidence] that God [who is deeply concerned about us] causes all things to work together [as a plan] for the good of those who love God, to those who are called according to His plan and purpose"* (AMP).

I don't know about you, but I find it comforting to know God has had a plan all along. He's always had a plan to bring you and me out of the bondage of whatever holds us back or holds us down. God has provided a plan to forgive us and afford us an eternal home that is greater than anything we can ever imagine. His plan also takes into consideration all the detours we'll take down the grocery store isles of life.

If you think about it, nothing you or I do will ever surprise God. Do you realize that? God is never surprised when you make the right call, the wrong call, or no call at all. In fact, He's known all along what choices you'd make. As such, He masterfully crafts each paragraph of your life, knowing exactly what characters and events to arrange and rearrange in your story. He knows how to work all things together to bring good out of bad and make the good even better. He already knows the detours we'll take and His roadside assistance plan always includes forgiveness and meaningful redirection.

Forgiveness: It's Yours For The Taking

Though the ransom has been paid and our detours have been taken into account, many of us live as though we are still under the constricting pressure of condemnation. God has forgiven us, but we can't seem to forgive ourselves.

When was the last time you spent hours, days, weeks, even years punishing yourself for something God has already forgiven you? The Apostle Paul, in his second letter to the Corinthian church, is definitive in saying there's a difference between worldly sorrow and Godly sorrow. In essence Paul says *worldly sorrow* is *regret* for getting caught, but *Godly sorrow* causes a change within us "and leaves *no regret*" (see 2 Corinthians 7:10, *emphasis mine*, NIV).

If you're truly sorry for your Complacency, Frustration, Independence, and Rebellious ways, yet you continue to beat yourself up with regret and shame, the feelings you have are a result of listening to the devil's accusations about you rather than the truth of God's grace. In *Fighting the Lies of the Enemy*—a free guided journal by Lysa TerKeurst and Proverbs 31 Ministries—Lysa declares this concerning the devil's lies: *"He comes in as a whisper, lingers like a gentle breeze, and builds like a storm you don't even see coming. He's not whispering his lies to coddle us. He wants to crush us."*[26]

The devil says one thing, but Jesus says another. Which will you choose to believe?

When asked what the greatest commandment of God is, Jesus replied by saying, "Love the Lord your God with all your heart and with all your soul and with all your mind and with all your strength" (Mark 12:30, NIV). Jesus went on to say there is a second commandment that is equally important. That commandment is to "Love your neighbor as yourself" (v.31, NIV). These two commands are recorded in the gospel accounts of both Mark and Matthew. In the Matthew account, Jesus adds, "All the Law and the Prophets hang on these two commandments (Matthew 22:40, NIV). In other words, everything God wants you to do or become in life depends on loving Him and loving others as you love yourself.

Notice there are three groupings of love we are to give. First, we are to fully love God. Secondly, we are to love others. The third love we are to have is often overlooked. We are also to love ourselves.

Sometimes loving ourselves seems like the hardest part. Maybe that's because we keep doing the same things we've always done. Maybe it's because we choose to listen to the devil's lies rather that the Truths of God. When this is the case, we're often prone to feel like we are always letting God and those we love down.

One of the most likely culprits that distorts and spoils our self-image is when we are caught up in our own spin cycle. During these moments of frustrated incomprehension, the answer is to simply cut our cycle short. We need to get back to a place of intimacy with God. A few questions you might ask yourself, if you are a person who continuously beats yourself up, are:

- When was the last time I pondered how truly great God is, even when I doubt His love?

- When was the last time I took the time—in full Surrender—to get on my knees and pray about my life circumstances? To pray for others?

- How long has it been since I made a list of the things I'm grateful for and thanked God for His intervention?

- How much time have I spent, lately, truly reflecting on God's Word (the Bible), His Truths, and His promises for my life in the moments when I am fully Surrendered to Him?

- Have I set up a *monument* to God's provision and intervention in my life, reminding me of His grace and goodness?

- If I've created a monument, how long has it been since I pondered the things represented there?

- When was the last time I asked for help and then fully Surrendered to God's unfailing Rescue?

If you're like me, you may look at this list of questions and begin to beat yourself up even more. You may realize you've been Complacent—or worse. In the midst of this realization, you may feel even more unworthy than before. May I remind you that God is never surprised by our actions? He already knows the ways in which you will miss the mark of His absolute best—today, tomorrow, and even how you missed a beat for His best for you yesterday.

The realization we must come to—instead of a constant analysis of our own failures—is that God doesn't deal as harshly with us as we often do ourselves. We habitually listen to the devil's lies and our own ingrained perceptions. We believe we'll never get it right, never become the person God desires, and that we will always let Him down. We can often let failures like these lead us to give up on ourselves. As a result—and on varying levels—our perception of ourselves impacts how we choose to love God and show love toward others. As defeated lies grow ever stronger in our hearts and minds, we may lose the ability to truly love others because we have lost the ability to love ourselves.

Without refute, our actions often let others down, even hurt them. But our actions are simply a reflection of our attitudes. If we truly believe we are loved by God, completely forgiven by Him, and have the ability—with His help—to become all He desires for us, our new attitude will greatly affect how we show genuine love and compassion toward others and toward God.

The question becomes, do we really believe these things about ourselves? Do you believe you are loved by God, without condition? Do you believe God knows your worst days and loves you anyway? Do you believe you are forgiven, even in the midst of your deepest depravities?

I love how one particular Biblical author addresses our inward insecurities:

> "There is no fear in love [dread does not exist]. But perfect (complete, full-grown) love drives out fear, because fear involves [the expectation of divine] punishment, so the one who is afraid [of God's judgment] is not perfected in love [has not grown into a sufficient understanding of God's love]" (1 John 4:18, AMP).

Perhaps your doubt of God's unconditional love causes you to fear Him and fear letting Him down. Perhaps you have not grown into "a sufficient understanding of God's love." If this is the case, rereading the chapter entitled "Who's Your Daddy?" will give you hope and strength to face your own inadequacies in the same way God does.

> "The Lord is compassionate and merciful, slow to get angry and filled with unfailing love. He will not

constantly accuse us, nor remain angry forever. He does not punish us for all our sins; he does not deal harshly with us, as we deserve... For he knows how weak we are..." (Psalm 103:8-10, 14a, NLT).

If you've placed your faith in Christ and believe in God's redemptive love, may I suggest you begin with the belief that's in your head and then let those same thoughts resonate into your heart? Begin by telling yourself *"If God already knows my weaknesses, and loves me anyway, I need to learn how to love myself the way He already loves me."*

Oddly enough, the word "if' in the Bible can often be translated as "since." With that in mind, after you've practiced saying the previous statement aloud for several days, try altering *two* words. Begin speaking the positivity of God's infallible love over yourself and your life circumstances by saying, "*Since* God already knows my weaknesses, and loves me anyway, I *choose* to learn how to love myself the way He already loves me."

This will take some contemplative practice. Only you, God, and the enemy of your soul know your deepest, darkest, secret habits and weaknesses. And, because it's often easier to believe the devil's accusations—instead of God's truthful promises—it may take weeks of speaking God's Truths over your life to overcome years of misguided lies the devil has engrained in your brain. But, once you've truly committed to loving yourself the way God loves you, your expressions of love toward others and your grateful love toward God will radically change the rest of your life.

I have a placard on my nightstand that says, "God Loves You and So Do I." Perhaps we should all have a plaque that slightly differs from my inscription. Instead, we should each have a framed version of "God Loves Me and So Do I." If we choose to take that concept to heart, each and every day, we will have the full capacity to live out the two greatest commandments God has ever given—love God and love others as we do ourselves.

Forgive: Pass It Along

In complete gratefulness to God, I have never had a loved one marred or murdered by someone else's selfish actions. Neither have I been so critically injured. With no doubt, I carry physical and emotional scars that give definition to who I am today. Still, I have no idea what it's like to have a loved one killed by a drunken or distracted driver. I don't know what it's like to have the knowledge of someone abusing my daughter or financially raping a loved one. I don't know what it's like to have a child so defiled by an addiction that they've stolen everything valuable to me—including my heart. If you know these feelings, the word forgiveness—especially as it relates to the person involved—may not be within your vocabulary.

I don't know if you are familiar with Anjelah Johnson's character, Bon Qui Qui on MADtv.[27] If not, do a simple search for "King Burger;" the scene is quite hilarious! In the sequence, when Bon Qui Qui is referring to a recent act of disrespect toward herself, she says, "I will cut him." Cutting someone does not even come close to the animosity I would feel toward someone who blatantly disrespected my daughter, let alone misaligned her life forever.

Perhaps you feel the same. Who could ever forgive someone who cheated on them, ran head-on into a loved one in a drunken state, robbed them of their livelihood, raped their daughter, or left their son with a permanent disability?

For some of us the assault is less obtrusive. Still, the invasion can be similarly disrespectful. "He lied to me." "She stabbed me in the back to get that promotion." "I trusted him with my heart; now I'm broken."

Where does it end? How can we forgive? We might even say, "I can forgive this person, but I will never forget." There may be some validity to that statement (we'll address that in a moment); but, have we ever truly forgiven the assailant of our sanity? If not, perhaps our unwillingness to forgive is the root of our insanity.

Consider this: Your misaligned decisions and impudent actions have already taken the life of someone. Because of poor judgements, mistakes, or all-out Rebellion, you took the life of God's very own Son. Worse than any perpetrator could devalue your life or the life of someone you love, you have already committed the same evil. Your sin cost God the life of His one and only Son. The difference is, God knew what He was getting into (costly plan) and loved you enough to allow His ultimate sacrifice to be a gift to you.

> "Get rid of all bitterness, rage, anger, harsh words, and slander, as well as all types of evil behavior. Instead, be kind to each other, tenderhearted, forgiving one another, *just as God through Christ has forgiven you*" (Ephesians 4:31-32, *emphasis mine*, NLT).

In my "I will cut him" mentality, forgiving *just as God has forgiven me* is often a concept that is simply thrown out of the window. But, living life without forgiveness is like dying from a venomous poison. The British novelist, Charlotte Bronte, says, "Something of vengeance I had tasted for the first time; as aromatic wine it seemed, on swallowing, warm and racy; its after-flavor, metallic and corroding, gave me a sensation as if I had been poisoned."[28] With this notion in mind, I've heard it said that harboring resentment or ill-will toward someone is like drinking poison and expecting the other person to die. That is so true! When we choose to hold another person's sin against them, it is our own souls that suffer. They may not even know they've wronged you. Or, they may know it, but rarely think of you or their actions. All the while, you allow yourself to become consumed.

Have you ever considered that you may have hurt or offended someone to the point that they are as consumed by you as you are by someone else's actions? Maybe you're the one who consumes their thoughts? We all sin. We all have times when our own self-centeredness has caused someone else pain. Yet, we feel like we are the ones who deserve to stand as judge and juror.

What if everyone you'd ever hurt rose up one day with a petition to convict you of your selfish "crimes"? What would be your sentence? Is it the same one you are wishing one someone else even now?

Perhaps that's why Jesus, while instructing His disciples—and us—on how to pray, He indicates that the forgiveness we ask for should be the kind of forgiveness we're willing to give (see the Lord's Prayer, Matthew 6:12). Jesus seems go into greater detail about forgiving our sins as we forgive those who sin against us with the following teaching:

> "Do not judge others, and you will not be judged. For you will be treated as you treat others. The standard you use in judging is the standard by which you will be judged. And why worry about a speck in your friend's eye when you have a log in your own? How can you think of saying to your friend, 'Let me help you get rid of that speck in your eye,' when you can't see past the log in your own eye? Hypocrite! First get rid of the log in your own eye; then you will see well enough to deal with the speck in your friend's eye" (Matthew 7:1-5, NLT).

This passage gives us a clear indication that if we want grace from others, we need to learn to be gracious. We are also given instruction about where our focus should be when it comes to faults. Rather than focusing our attention on the errors of others, we need to consider our own personal deficiencies and attend to those things first. In essence, Jesus teaches us in this passage that instead of making it our singular purpose in life to make sure people know how they've harmed us, our greatest focus should be gracious living, accompanied by personal growth.

But what about those people who grate every nerve in our body? Those people who continue to harm us, bring us trouble, or who are simply a menace? *Jesus says we are to forgive them as well.*

In fact, one of Jesus' disciples must have been struggling with the whole concept of forgiving such a person when he asked Jesus, *"Lord, how often should I forgive someone who sins against me? Seven times?"* (Matthew 21:18b, NLT). Seven times seems more than adequate for me to forgive someone who continues to usher pain into my life, but Jesus responds by saying, "No, not seven times, but seventy times seven" (see Matthew 18:22, NLT).

I don't want to get stuck on semantics, but some translations simply say seventy times. Still, if this translation is correct, seventy times seven equals 490 times. Truthfully, I've harmed the same person in similar ways more than 490 times. So, is that the limit? I hope not!

In the Bible, the number seven is considered to be a number of perfection or completion. As such, Jesus is saying that we should forgive people an infinite number of times. In a similar teaching, found in Luke 17:3-4, Jesus indicates our forgiveness of others should be infinite, even if this seeming nuisance keeps repeating the same hurtful misgivings multiple times every single day.

I have to say that this teaching is a hard pill for me to swallow. I want others to forgive me innumerous times each day, but I don't have the mental or emotional energy to be infinitely forgiving—for the same things—day after day.

Take a deep breath and absorb all of what Jesus is teaching. Start with the deep breath and then consider how many times you make mistakes or even make intentional digs on any given day. Your actions may not be overt. Instead, they may be disguised by backhanded comments. Still, you need forgiveness more than seven times a day. I do too. And, so do they.

If we look back at the Matthew 7 passage, we see that grace is received when grace is given. We also see that we need to focus on our own issues rather than constantly finding fault in others. What's just as intriguing about Jesus' teaching in this passage is the verse that comes next:

> "Don't waste what is holy on people who are unholy.
> Don't throw your pearls to pigs! They will trample the
> pearls, then turn and attack you" (Matthew 7:6, NLT).

Just as living a life of resentment and considering some people as unworthy of forgiveness is poisonous to our individual souls, there are also people whose toxic nature should be avoided at all cost! They are like pigs which will turn on us and trample us.

Don't forget that this teaching of Jesus immediately follows His indications of forgiving in the same way we would like to be forgiven and His implications of judging others. Yet Jesus tells us just a few verses later that *"By their fruit you will recognize them. Do people pick grapes from thornbushes, or figs from thistles? Likewise, every good tree bears good fruit, but a bad tree bears bad fruit. A good tree cannot bear bad fruit, and a bad tree cannot bear good fruit"* (Matthew 7:16-17, NIV).

We cannot judge people's hearts or motives. Jesus is clear on this. If we do, the same nature of judgement will fall upon us. However, Scripture should always be taken in context. Jesus tells us that, though we are not worthy of the position of judge and jury when it comes to a person's heart, we can be confident in assuming someone's general nature by the way they consistently act and react. Some people are just poisonous. As such, we should forgive them, but also avoid them—at all costs.

I have been that person who was toxic to everyone around me. Maybe you have been too. The key is to cut your cycle short, discover and learn to live in *God's Sweet Spot*, and Trust that God is the ultimate, forgiving judge. Your life, and the lives around you, will be changed because you know God to be forgiving, you choose to accept His forgiveness, choose to forgive yourself, and stop being so hard on others who are struggling with the same spin cycle you've been on for far too long.

Selah (Pause for Reflection)

Take *15 Minutes* and Make this Chapter *Personal*

> *NOTE: Always keep a Bible, notebook, and pen ready.*
> ***Why?*** *I believe God will open himself up to you during this time of reflection, just as He does for me.*

All I have is a big *sigh* at the end of this chapter. Forgiveness is difficult to receive and to give. Grace is the greatest thing any of us can glean from this chapter. We don't deserve it; neither do those who have done us wrong. But, grace isn't something we earn or deserve. It's a gift. Are you willing to give and receive this wonderful possession?

> "For it is by grace you have been saved, through faith— and this is not from yourselves, it is the gift of God" (Ephesians 2:8, NIV).

Prayer:

> *"Thank You, God, for loving me, forgiving me, and for offering Your grace and forgiveness to me as a gift. Please help me to show others the same grace you have so freely given to me. I know this will help me love You, others, and myself in the ways You earnestly desire. In Jesus' name, please help me move forward in the ways of forgiveness. Amen."*

Chapter Twenty

FINDING YOUR WAY

"The Lord is my shepherd; I shall not want. He makes me lie down in green pastures. He leads me beside still waters. He restores my soul. He leads me in paths of righteousness for his name's sake."
~ Psalm 23:1-3, ESV

I have an affinity for water. I love the vast expanse and mysteries of the ocean. I've hiked for miles on end to take in the majesty of a waterfall. I enjoy quarries, ponds, lakes, rivers—especially whitewater rafting—and babbling brooks. In humorous humility, the little boy in me is even drawn to large puddles. Something inside me just wants to jump in and make a splash.

Thanks, in part, to the way too many water-creature movies I have seen, I am not fond of water I can't see through. I don't know what's in there, and that is when my mind goes back to the movies I have seen. One that really freaked me out was 20th Century Fox's 1999 movie *Lake Placid*. In the film, a mutated crocodile—the size of a cargo truck—struck enough fear in me to become the predominant reason why I don't get more than ankle-deep in water I can't see through.

Finding Your Way

As I look back on the chronicles of this book, I recall my "safari blues" in the *If God Really Cared About Me* chapter. A friend of mine had gone on safari and had taken some truly breathtaking pictures. One of those pictures was of a giraffe taking a life-sustaining drink of water from the still waters of a South African watering hole. The giraffe's long neck was stooped as it silently lapped a refreshing drink. If you recall the story, the picture's most amazing quality was the reflection of the giraffe in the water beneath it.

Bam! All I can picture is the crocodile from *Lake Placid* leaping from the murky waters and latching itself onto the stately neck of this beautiful giraffe. And, yes; crocodiles are native to this area of Africa.

There are times when that's the way we view life, ourselves, and the circumstances life brings. Life seems to have settled down. We're enjoying a fresh drink and relaxing in a greeting-card moment, when all of a sudden we find ourselves ensnared in the same thing we thought we'd found the strength to overcome. The caption of our card changes from "Thank You God" to "Why Does This Keep Happening To Me?"

If you haven't caught on by now, dissecting what's commonly referred to as the *Lord's Prayer* has been a consistent theme throughout the working part of this book.

> "Our Father in heaven, hallowed be your name. Your kingdom come, your will be done, on earth as it is in heaven. Give us this day our daily bread, and forgive us our debts [meaning, sins or trespasses], as we also have forgiven our debtors [those who sin or trespass against us]. And lead us not into temptation, but deliver us from evil. *For yours is the kingdom and the power and the glory, forever. Amen" (Matthew 6:9-13, [bracketed]

notes mine, *not included in all ancient manuscripts of the original language, ESV).

As a part of Jesus' teaching on prayer, He said we are to ask God to "Lead us not into temptation, but deliver us from evil..." (Matthew 6:13a). I've always been confused by this teaching because the Bible says that God does not tempt anyone (see James 1:13-15). As I've studied the Bible, the original languages, and the context of particular verses, I've learned that a better translation of Jesus' instruction in this prayer is simply, "lead us away from temptation." In effect, we're asking God to show us a better way by saying "Don't let me go *there* again."

A Better Way

In the opening of this chapter, I quoted the first three verses of a well-known Scripture in Psalm 23. The entirety of the passage says:

> "¹The Lord is my shepherd; I shall not want. ²He makes me lie down in green pastures. He leads me beside still waters. ³He restores my soul. He leads me in paths of righteousness for his name's sake. ⁴Even though I walk through the valley of the shadow of death, I will fear no evil, for you are with me; your rod and your staff, they comfort me. ⁵You prepare a table before me in the presence of my enemies; you anoint my head with oil; my cup overflows. ⁶Surely goodness and mercy shall follow me all the days of my life, and I shall dwell in the house of the Lord forever" (Psalm 23:1-6, ESV).

I could write a whole series of books on this one passage; but, the best summary of this wonderful promise of God can be found in a few clarifying statements:

1) In verse one, the defining element is that God is our shepherd. He takes care of us, leads us, keeps us under his personal protection, and always provides for our basic needs;

2) Verse two tells us that there are times when we need a break. Usually we don't recognize the need ourselves. Instead, we push ourselves beyond physical and mental limitations. God, however, knows what's best for us and intentionally slows us down from time to time. He knows we need rest. We may not understand why things aren't moving forward, but He does. Additionally, an understanding of the *still* water is critical to this verse. Is it easier to drink from a steadied cup or from a water fountain? How about from a babbling brook? God has the ability to bring us to planned places where we can find rest and absorb His peaceful, *still* replenishment;

3) The third verse reiterates the previous, but adds some definition. God does all the things He does in our lives to bring us to a place of restoration. God's intervention on our lives is a clarifying notice that He is a loving and graceful God who has purposes for us that are greater than what we can imagine;

4) There will be critical times in our lives when we're not sure if God is on our side, or even present. In verse four, God reassures us that even when times are tough, He's there. Not only is God there, He's also brought with Him two tools that will help us. The first is protective. God brings a "rod" to keep predators away. His *rod* is for our Rescue. His staff can be a bit more intrusive, however. Though not always, God's staff may be a measure of discipline. Even so, His staff is for guiding, not for snagging us or ruling over our actions. Instead, His staff is a measure for keeping us on the right path and for helping us cut our cycle short;

5) Verse five tells us that even when we are in a place of open vulnerability—where those who see us as prey, know our every weakness, and seek the opportunity to capitalize on that susceptibility—God already has a plan to make sure things turn out for our best. In fact, anointing the head of a sheep with oil keeps predators—even hidden ones, like snakes in a hole—from attacking. The oil, poured on the head of a sheep and down the holes of possible predators, keeps sheep safe from attack. In the darkest of places or the greenest of pastures, it may not always seem like God has our back; but, He does. And our cup will always be (more than) half full if we choose to let our Shepherd lead and protect us;

6) Just reread verse six and accept it. The sooner you do, the more clarity you'll have in seeing how God is always leading us away from temptation and toward His absolute best for our lives.

Those six verses are defining. They discern who God is and bring clarity to where He desires to lead us. God does not lead us into temptation, Frustration, or an empty, dry land of Complacency. God's desire is to lead each of us into a place of fullness, protected prosperity, safety, Surrendered obedience, goodness, mercy, and—ultimately—into His *Sweet Spot*.

Perhaps you'll want to read and reread the passage and the clarifying statements above. How does Psalm 23 and its implications apply to where you are now, the place you want to be, and the *Sweet Spot* you want to continuously live in?

A Defining Moment

A friend of mine had a defining moment a little over 12 years ago. She determined to accept God's unconditional love for her and began believing His promises—like the ones in Psalm 23—were true for her life. She decided to believe that God's promises were more than just words from an ancient religious document; instead, they were declarative Truths over her life!

For anonymity's sake, we'll call my friend *Kim*. Kim had been struggling with a particular debilitating behavior for many years. Kim grew up in church. Despite her religious background, however, Kim only knew of religion. She'd never truly experienced what it meant to have a relationship with God. The Rescue from her Rebellion was always at her fingertips, but freedom cannot be found in religion. It can only be found in an intimate, Trusting relationship with God.

After choosing to replace religion with a genuine relationship with the lover of her soul, Kim began to grow in her faith. On this wonderful journey, Kim discovered a promise from God that altered her path and changed her life. She'd already been forgiven, but this one verse set her on a pathway to complete Surrender. This Scripture coincides with everything that *Learning to Live in God's Sweet Spot* represents. And, it gave her freedom she'd been searching for her whole life:

> "The temptations in your life are no different from what others experience. And God is faithful. *He will not allow the temptation to be more than you can stand. When you are tempted, he will show you a way out* so that you can endure" (1 Corinthians 10:13, *emphasis mine*, NLT).

What's Your Moment?

Maybe your moment is when you finally decide to let your family be the number-one priority in your life, instead of your career. Perhaps, your moment is when you discover a family member—even your child or spouse—has an incurable disease. Your moment may not come until you're behind bars, bankrupt, the secretary finally decides to break silence about the affair you're having, you siphon the family's emergency fund for your own "need," or when you begin seeing everything around you as a liability instead of an asset.

Maybe the credit card is overdue, again. My payment due on Kohl's, Macy's, or my—otherwise—etcetera bill is WAY over my family's budget. My overpriced coffee, tea, and my unplanned bill on Etsy is way unexplained. I make excuses—every way I can—but; I am simply overdue. Now what?

As I've mentioned before, addiction has often been my nemesis. But isn't it everyone's? *What's yours?* The first things seem obvious: drugs, alcohol, pornography, sex. But what about shopping, adrenaline, food, or whatever your secret or selfish desire? Whatever ensnares you, defeats you! Don't let anything that seems to have power over you become your "god." There's always a way out!

> *"...When you are tempted, he will show you a way out* so that you can endure" (1 Corinthians 10:13b, NLT).

The Way Out

First and foremost, your freedom and the fulfilled promise of a life that is overflowing and free of regret depends on cutting your cycle short. When was the last time you got on your knees in serious, dedicated prayer? How much time have you spent, lately, in contemplative meditation on God's Word? Have you made a gratitude list or added anything to your monument of God's goodness lately? Are you holding any grudges? Are you actively looking for God's way or are you doing things the way you've always done them? Where are you in your cycle?

Those are questions I always begrudge, at first. Then, after a moment of contemplation, I have to face the reality of where I'm living. Am I in a rut or am I living God's best for my life at this moment? Where am I in my cycle? Since God always provides a way out, in what way is God currently offering an escape for you? A way to cut your cycle short?

A sponsor in an addictive rehabilitation program always used to tell me, "Daron, if you don't drink today, you're not going to explode." How does that translate for you and your current circumstances? Maybe for you it's, "If I get some Biblical, Christian counseling, I can learn to love myself in the same way God loves me... and I won't explode." Maybe during your current journey into *God's Sweet Spot* you'll discover that you won't burst into flames if you choose to respond to your spouse's disrespect with loving kindness instead of tit-for-tat. Spontaneous combustion also doesn't occur if you choose to spend wisely instead of impulsively buying the next greatest thing. I promise, whatever the fashion statement, automobile upgrade, or technological wonder, it isn't going to make you feel any better about yourself. In the same way, undermining someone's efforts at work is not going to send you on the fast-track to success. And, maybe—just maybe—a few words of encouragement to someone you care about won't cause your inflated ego to burst. Or, maybe it will; and, you'll be better off because you discover what it means to be a man or woman of humility and respect.

Maybe you need to quit your job (finding another financially responsible position, first, is always recommended). Maybe you need someone in your life who is not willing to accept your bull anymore. And, in due respect, you need to learn to listen to that person. Maybe you need to swallow your pride and go to rehab (again). Or, maybe you don't think you need anything. Even *that* is a place to start. It's a place I found myself recently.

Maybe You're In the Same Place As I Am

I've talked a lot about finding joy and fulfillment. In fact, in the opening text of this book I emphatically stated that I am in a better place than I've ever been. And, for the most part, I am. However, I recently came to the realization—as I'm nearing the end of chronicling what I believe God inspired me to write—that I haven't been experiencing much joy or fulfillment lately. Instead, I've been anxious about finances and the particulars of how to get this book published.

In my "aha" moment, I realized that if I'm anxious, then I'm not in a Trusting place with God. So, where am I in my cycle? During this epiphany, I realized I've been Complacent and Frustrated instead of joyously fulfilled.

I've read and studied God's Word for the purposes of writing this book; but, I haven't been meditating on these same words for the pure joy of getting to know God better. In my heart I know I need to find joy in getting to know God better so I can Trust and love Him more. I know this is the only pathway to fulfillment and finding contentment in Him alone.

Sometimes the way God leads us away from temptation—or simply to a better place—is by prompting us in our spirits to do something different. This morning I woke up and decided I was going to be joyful again. My decision was not because I didn't want to experience joy all along, but because God prompted my heart by reminding me there's a better way. The way God has shown me throughout writing this book, however, is a choice.

I had to decide today that I was going to stop writing and reread the instructions God has already given me on living a life of joy and fulfillment. If you've gotten this far in reading God's instructions for a better life and you're not experiencing what you've read, perhaps you need to stop, reread, and begin practicing what you've read. This book is inspired, and it works... if you choose to work it!

The best part of practicing what I'm writing (what you're reading) is not just that your life will get better. The greater result is that the lives of people around you will be restored as well. God's goodness will be magnified because you choose to do something different today. We choose a different way because it brings glory to God. And, the result is that by choosing the *Sweet Spot* of Trusting God—in complete Surrender—the essence of Psalm 23 becomes a reality:

> "He leads me in paths of righteousness for his name's sake... Surely goodness and mercy shall follow me all the days of my life, and I shall dwell in the house [*The Sweet Spot*] of the Lord forever" (Psalm 23:3b, 6 [*bracketed*] note mine, ESV).

Selah (Pause for Reflection)

Take *15 Minutes* and Make this Chapter *Personal*

> *NOTE: Always keep a Bible, notebook, and pen ready.* **Why?** *I believe God will open himself up to you during this time of reflection, just as He does for me.*

Are you *Learning to Live in God's Sweet Spot* or are you still an empty mess? Perhaps reflecting on a few of the nuggets of wisdom, found throughout this book, will give you some encouragement to stay strong, follow though, and keep taking baby steps into *God's Sweet Spot*:

- Say aloud, "I have hopeful expectation for my life because I have restful confidence in God's plan for my future."

- Pray, "Father God, I don't always recognize my own, personal failings—emotionally, mentally, financially, strategically, relationally, or otherwise. Please impress upon my heart the often unnoticed patterns in my life that are keeping me from experiencing Your absolute best. I also know there are obvious repetitions in my behavior that urgently need transformation. I don't want to be controlled by my own imprudent ways. Instead, I desire to be guided and cleansed by living in the refuge of Your grace and presence. Please show me each of my unhealthy patterns and help me live the kind of life that is evident of peace, grace, and complete fulfillment. In Jesus' name I pray these things become true in my life; amen."

- Say aloud, "I am content with my life. I know God loves me and desires what's best for me. I fully trust God and His purposes for my life. I have begun to see my life and the world around me as beautiful."

- Pray, "Father God, I pray that from the depths of Your glorious and unlimited resources, You will empower me—deep within—with the kind of inner strength that only You can provide. Through Your Holy Spirit, I pray you lift me up, prepare me, and strengthen me for everything ahead of me today. In Jesus' name I ask these things; amen."

- Pray, "...Help me overcome my unbelief" (Mark 9:24b, NIV).

- Pray, "I have carried this burden for too long. I am not capable of enduring the weight it's bringing on me. I give it to You, God, and Trust You to take it from me. In Jesus name, set me free; amen."

- Accept the fact that "...We know that God causes everything to work together for the good of those who love God and are called according to his purpose for them" (Romans 8:28, NLT).

- Pray, "Since God already knows my weaknesses, and loves me anyway, I choose to learn how to love myself the way He already loves me."

Chapter Twenty-One

LIVING LIFE ON PURPOSE

"The mystery of human existence lies not in just staying alive, but in finding something to live for."
~ *Fyodor Dostoyevsky, The Brothers Karamazov*[29]

What is it you want most out of life? Take a moment and dream a little. If you could have, become, or accomplish certain things in life what would they be? Maybe you could list five, ten, maybe even fifteen things you'd consider defining.

I know my list. I don't even have to think twice. I want my daughter to love me and find joy in being with me. I want her to learn to respect me as a loving father. I want her—no matter her age or stage in life—to look at me with admiration and love in her eyes and proudly declare, "That's my dad!"

Though I'm in no hurry, I'd like to remarry someday. I want to be the kind of man that treats his wife with respect and honor. I want to finally be in a relationship where I'm not draining the life out of the woman I love. Instead, I want to be a man who sacrificially fills my wife with love, kindness, generosity, and tenderheartedness.

I want to become the kind of man whose life is lived in such a way that people want what I have. Not in a coveting, jealous, way, but in a way where people can see the love of God exuding through my attitudes and actions. I want others to see that I'm living in *God's Sweet Spot* and desire to learn what I've learned.

I want to be the kind of man who is compassionate, generous, and appreciative of those around me—whether friends, family, neighbors, or complete strangers. I want to treat others as I want to be treated (see Matthew 7:12).

I want to become a bestselling author and speaker. I want to teach the precepts of this book and see people's lives radically changed. I want to see people living in God's fullness and fully living out His purpose for their lives.

There is, however, one condition for me—or you—to see all of our Godly desires become a reality. To become the dad, husband, friend, and influencer I want to be, I cannot just read the words contained in this book. I must live them. For you to become all God desires you to be and to live in *God's Sweet Spot*, you must too.

The Fullness Of Our Journey

The latter portion of this book has been based, in part, on the Lord's Prayer (see Matthew 6:9-13). This is how I learned the Lord's Prayer as a child and how I say it today:

> Our Father, who art in heaven,
> hallowed be thy Name,
> thy kingdom come,
> thy will be done,
> on earth as it is in heaven.

> Give us this day our daily bread.
> And forgive us our trespasses,
> as we forgive those
> who trespass against us.
> And lead us not into temptation,
> but deliver us from evil.
> For thine is the kingdom,
> and the power, and the glory,
> for ever and ever. Amen.[30]

Instead of the Frustrated emptiness most people—Christians included—experience, I want to live a life of fulfillment, joy, peace, and Trust in God. I want to consistently live in the "secret place" (see Psalm 91:1, KJV) of *God's Sweet Spot*.

In order to dwell in that blissful place, I need to evaluate where I am in the spin cycle of Trust, Complacency, Frustration, Independence, Rebellion, Trouble. Only then can I cut my cycle short by Surrendering myself to God's best on a day-to-day, minute-by-minute basis. He will always come to my Rescue when I am fully Surrendered to Him. When my arms are fully extended toward God, I will always find myself in a place of genuine Trust and be in His *Sweet Spot*. Learning to "Pray, Pray, Pray," especially the Lord's Prayer will always lead me to that place.

❖ *Our Father, Who Art In Heaven*

Is God your "Father"? If not, place your faith in the One True God, the God of heaven and earth. Stop believing the devil, who is the "father of lies." The devil wants to deceive you by telling you that you'll always end up in the same old rut. He wants to steal, kill, and destroy any hope you have for a better future. BUT GOD wants you to know that He has a better plan for your life and wants to give you a life overflowing with joy, peace, contentment, and Trust (see John 10:10 and Jeremiah 29:11).

❖ **Hallowed Be Thy Name**

Begin living a life that reflects an "attitude of gratitude." Make a list of all the ways God has been good to you. Every time you feel yourself getting Frustrated, make a list of at least ten things your grateful for. Build your "monument" to God of all the ways He's come through for you in tough circumstances. Honoring God for who He is will always cut your cycle short.

❖ **Thy Kingdom Come, Thy Will Be Done & Our Daily Bread**

Learn to know God and His will for your life by spending time reading, studying, and meditating on God's Word. Though you should always feel free to ask God for your needs, "give us this day our daily bread," the Bible is the *bread of life* (see Matthew 4:4). So, "Read, Read, Read." By getting to know God better, you will be able to discern His will for your life and you will learn to Trust Him more. As you grow in Trust, you will also learn to love God more and find contentment in Him, even in Troublesome times.

❖ **Forgive Us Our Trespasses...**

God went to great lengths to offer you a full pardon from your Rebellious ways. Though He may not always Rescue you from your circumstances, He has provided a means of being forgiven for your sins by offering Himself—in the form of Jesus—as the ultimate sacrifice for your sins. Accept that forgiveness, learn to forgive yourself, and extend that same grace to others.

❖ **Lead Us... And Deliver Us From Evil**

God's guidance, as found in His Word, will always lead you along the best path. Even when things seem dark or Troublesome, God is always at work to bring good out of your circumstances. Even when you are tempted to return to your Rebellious ways, God always has an alternative plan and will provide you with the strength to follow Him (see Psalm 23: 1-6, Romans 8:28, and 1 Corinthians 10:13). Follow God and take the way out!

The Missing Piece(s)

Have you ever completed a jigsaw puzzle? I've put together some pretty elaborate ones. I have one that was 2000 pieces. Put together, it stands 42.5 inches tall and is 34 inches wide. It's framed and behind glass. It was a very difficult puzzle to put together as it consisted primarily of only four colors.

If you've ever had a cat, a dog, or a toddler, you know how easy it is for even one piece to go missing. Can you imagine working on a 2000 piece puzzle, only to find there was a piece missing?

I have to admit this was devious, and I apologize for my scandalous actions, but I have helped friends work on puzzles before and intentionally taken a piece home with me so I could be the one who finished the puzzle. As I said, I have turned from my Rebellious ways. As such, I want to reveal to you the missing pieces.

Some older manuscripts of the Bible (in their original language) include a piece of the Lord's Prayer that others do not. As you read the Lord's Prayer (see Matthew 6:9-13), there is a part that's included in the version I learned as a child, but is missing from many modern translations of the Bible. If not included in the actual text, there will be a footnote for verse 13 that indicates a missing piece. The footnote will say that some manuscripts of the Lord's Prayer include "For thine is the kingdom, and the power, and the glory, for ever. Amen" (see verse

Matthew 6:13, KJV). Those words are the missing pieces to our pattern puzzle. They will ensure our ability to live in—and stay in—*God's Sweet Spot*.

We can take all the drastic measures and baby steps outlined in this book and be well on our way to God's best laid plans for our lives. Even so, we will find ourselves just a few steps from God's absolute best. I don't know about you, but I don't want to get 50 feet from home and run out of gas. These final three pieces will put our puzzle together and keep our tanks full for the entire journey.

❖ ***For Thine Is The Kingdom***

Oh, to be king or queen for a day; wouldn't that be nice? My corrupt way of thinking says that if I could be king for a day, everyone would be subject to my needs. In God's kingdom, things are different, however. God is the "King of kings and the Lord of lords" (see Revelation 19:16). But His Kingdom isn't about being served; it's about serving others (see Matthew 20:28). As such, to live life on purpose and find joy, peace, and contentment along the way, we must choose a life of service to others.

Living in *God's Sweet Spot*—His kingdom—and seeing His kingdom flourish in and around us, depends on us serving others and sharing what we're learning with others.

> "All praise to God, the Father of our Lord Jesus Christ. God is our merciful Father and the source of all comfort. He comforts us in all our troubles so that we can comfort others. When they are troubled, we will be able to give them the same comfort God has given us" (1 Corinthians 1:3-4, NLT).

Choosing to live in and live out God's kingdom will bring you much joy and fulfillment. Trying to establish your own kingdom will continue to leave you *run-out-of-gas, completely bone-dry, dead-on empty.* The choice is yours. Sharing what God is teaching you and what He is doing in your life may be the difference between *the frustration of running-on-empty* and *the fulfillment of life overflowing*. It's God's kingdom, but it's yours to give.

❖ For Ever and Ever

Has anyone ever told you they would "always" be there for you? I'm guessing you've discovered the same truth I have. That person let you down and you probably don't even talk anymore. Maybe someone—perhaps that same person—has also told you they would "never" lie to you? Guess what? That statement was a lie. How about, "I will love you forever and ever"?

I've been let down and let others down so many times in my life that I often find it hard to trust. But, in the final notes of the Lord's Prayer, we're told that the promises of God, and His definitive work in our lives, are forever True. God will *always* love us, desire the best for us, and work things out for our, ultimate, good. And, God will *never* turn His back on a Surrendered heart. In fact, if we seek Him will all of our hearts, there's a promise that we will be set free from whatever has been holding us captive or keeping us down:

> "'For I know the plans I have for you,' declares the Lord, 'plans to prosper you and not to harm you, plans to give you hope and a future. Then you will call on me and come and pray to me, and I will listen to you. You will seek me and find me when you seek me with all your heart. I will be found by you,' declares the Lord,

'and will bring you back from captivity...'" (Jeremiah 29:11-14a, NIV).

❖ *Amen*

We often hear or say the word "Amen" at the end of a prayer. But, what does it mean? My best translation is "So let it be." In effect, we're asking God—even declaring—that what we've just prayed will come to fruition.

In order to fully realize the journey we're on as one of fruitfulness and fulfilment we need to continually let the things we're learning become a daily reality in our lives. There's a gap between who you were when you began this journey toward *Learning to Live in God's Sweet Spot* and who you are now. Have an attitude of gratitude about that gap. There is also a gap between who you are now and who God, ultimately, wants you to become. That's your growth gap. In order to live in and stay in the sweetest of life's emotional, spiritual, and physical best, growth is of utmost importance. And, in order to grow, we must continue the practices outlined in this book *every day*.

Every day we need to take a self-inventory of where we are in our spin cycle. If we are anywhere besides a place of full Surrender and Trust, our next step is to turn around, cut our cycle short, and get back into *God's Sweet Spot*. As soon as you realize you're not praying, reading, growing, living a life a gratitude, are holding grudges, or are giving into your old ways of doing things, cut your cycle short and go back home.

"Amen" is not an ending to a prayer. It's asking for a continuation of your petitions. This book is not one you'll read once and instantaneously become fully healed. Instead, this book is one you'll read and reread as you find yourself becoming Complacent, Frustrated, Independent, Rebellious, or in Trouble (once again). This is a book you'll want to keep and, also, give away. In that way, God's kingdom—His *Sweet Spot*—will come into your life and grow into the lives of those around you.

May His kingdom (*Sweet Spot*) come! So let it be!

Selah (Pause for Reflection)

Take *15 Minutes* and Make this Chapter *Personal*

> *NOTE: Always keep a Bible, notebook, and pen ready.*
> ***Why?*** *I believe God will open himself up to you during this time of reflection, just as He does for me.*

In what ways can you begin living life on purpose? This is an essential Selah-Vie. The decision to reflect on your current path, God's best for you, and your purpose of sharing God's kingdom is a critical, life-changing moment.

- Take just a few moments and write down where you feel you are in your own cycle;

- Journal about what you're learning, and what you need to begin doing to cut your cycle short;

- Write a list of people who might benefit from your current journey into *God's Sweet Spot*;

- Make a commitment to share where you are and what you're learning with at least one other person this week. Though you will definitely want to keep your copy of this book, perhaps you could purchase a few copies for people whom you know are *running on empty*;

- Finally, still your heart, mind, and soul. Then read and claim the promises of God for those who choose to live in the secret place of *God's Sweet Spot*:

Psalm 91

¹"He who dwells in the secret place of the Most High shall remain stable and fixed under the shadow of the Almighty [Whose power no foe can withstand]. ²I will say of the Lord, He is my Refuge and my Fortress, my God; on Him I lean and rely, and in Him I [confidently] trust! ³For [then] He will deliver you from the snare of the fowler and from the deadly pestilence. ⁴[Then] He will cover you with His pinions, and under His wings shall you trust and find refuge; His truth and His faithfulness are a shield and a buckler. ⁵You shall not be afraid of the terror of the night, nor of the arrow (the evil plots and slanders of the wicked) that flies by day, ⁶Nor of the pestilence that stalks in darkness, nor of the destruction and sudden death that surprise and lay waste at noonday. ⁷A thousand may fall at your side, and ten thousand at your right hand, but it shall not come near you. ⁸Only a spectator shall you be [yourself inaccessible in the secret place of the Most High] as you witness the reward of the wicked. ⁹Because you have made the Lord your refuge, and the Most High your dwelling place, ¹⁰there shall no evil befall you, nor any plague or calamity come near your tent. ¹¹For He will give His angels [especial] charge over you to accompany and defend and preserve you in all your ways [of obedience and service]. ¹²They shall bear you up on their hands, lest you dash your foot against a stone. ¹³You shall tread upon the lion and adder; the young lion and the serpent shall you trample underfoot. ¹⁴Because he has set his love upon Me, therefore will I deliver him; I will set him on high, because he knows and understands My name [has a personal knowledge of My mercy, love,

and kindness—trusts and relies on Me, knowing I will never forsake him, no, never]. ¹⁵He shall call upon Me, and I will answer him; I will be with him in trouble, I will deliver him and honor him. ¹⁶With long life will I satisfy him and show him My salvation" (Psalm 91:1-16, AMPC).

This is God's promise to you. So let it be!

ENDNOTES

1. Goodreads.com. (n.d.). A quote from Meditations. [online] Available at: https://www.goodreads.com/quotes/698243-do-not-think-that-what-is-hard-for-you-to [Accessed 19 Jan. 2019].

2. Moore, B. (2007). *Get Out Of That Pit: Straight Talk About God's Deliverance*. Integrity Publishers.

3. Crowder, David. "All My Hope." All My Hope. sixstepsrecords/Sparrow Records. 2017. CD.

4. Wisdom Quotes. (n.d.). Those who cannot learn from history are doomed to repeat it. George Santanaya. [online] Available at: http://wisdomquotes.com/learn-from-history-george-santayana/ [Accessed 19 Jan. 2019].

5. Klove.com. [online].

6. MercyMe. "Dear Younger Me." Welcome to the New. Fair Trade/Columbia. 2014. CD.

7. Historians.org. (n.d.). Why Study History? | AHA. [online] Available at: https://www.historians.org/teaching-and-learning/why-study-history [Accessed 19 Jan. 2019].

8. Inc.com. (n.d). 30 Quotes on Trust That Will Make You Think. [online] Available at: https://www.inc.com/lolly-daskal/trust-me-these-30-quotes-about-trust-could-make-a-huge-difference.html [Accessed 19 Jan. 2019].

9. Crosswalk.com. (2019). Grow in Faith with Daily Christian Living Articles. [online] Available at: https://www.crosswalk.com/newsletters-only/loving-actions/ [Accessed 19 Jan. 2019].

10. BrainyQuote. (n.d.). Scott Hamilton Quotes. [online] Available at: https://www.brainyquote.com/quotes/scott_hamilton_104173 [Accessed 19 Jan. 2019].

[11] A-Z Quotes. (n.d.). TOP 10 QUOTES BY RESHAD FEILD | A-Z Quotes. [online] Available at: https://www.azquotes.com/author/27744-Reshad_Feild [Accessed 19 Jan. 2019].

[12] Goodreads.com. (n.d.). A quote from Making Wishes. [online] Available at: https://www.goodreads.com/quotes/1286047-it-is-a-difficult-thing-if-not-impossible-to-forgive-oneself-for [Accessed 19 Jan. 2019].

[13] Goodreads.com. (n.d.). A quote from The Merchant of Death. [online] Available at: https://www.goodreads.com/quotes/129078-whenever-you-look-back-and-say-if-you-know-you-re [Accessed 19 Jan. 2019].

[14] Brainyquote.com. (n.d.). William Boothe Quotes. [online] Available at: https://www.brainyquote.com/quotes/william_booth_158774 [Accessed 19 Jan. 2019].

[15] "Might Mouse." Peter Pan Record. Terrytoon Studios. 20th Century Fox. 1962.

[16] "The Wizard of Oz." New York. MGM/UA. 1939.

[17] Brainyquote.com. (n.d.). George Washington Quotes. [online] Available at: https://www.brainyquote.com/quotes/george_washington_122875158774 [Accessed 19 Jan. 2019].

[18] "What about Bob?" United States: Buena Vista Pictures Distribution, Inc., 1991.

[19] Goodreads.com. (n.d.). A quote by Abraham Lincoln. [online] Available at: https://www.goodreads.com/quotes/38057-i-have-been-driven-many-times-upon-my-knees-by [Accessed 19 Jan. 2019].

[20] Smalley, Gary, and Norma Smalley. It Takes Two to Tango: More than 250 Secrets to Communication, Romance and Intimacy in Marriage. Colorado Springs, CO: Focus on the Family, 1997.

[21] Tomilin, Chris. "Good Good Father." Never Lose Sight. sixstepsrecords/Sparrow Records. 2015. CD

[22] Brainyquote.com. (n.d.). John F. Kennedy Quotes. [online] Available at: https://www.brainyquote.com/quotes/john_f_kennedy_105511 [Accessed 19 Jan. 2019].

[23] Gaither, Bill, and Gloria Gaither. "Because He Lives." Because He Lives. Spring House Music Group. 2005. CD.

[24] Stewart, J. (n.d.). The Refuge | Daily Declarations. [online] Therefuge.net. Available at: https://www.therefuge.net/resources/daily-declarations.html [Accessed 19 Jan. 2019].

[25] Goodreads.com. (n.d.). A quote from Waldmeer. [online] Available at: https://www.goodreads.com/quotes/8596409-every-grievance-you-hold-hides-a-little-more-of-the [Accessed 19 Jan. 2019].

[26] Go.lysaterkeurst.com. (2019). Fighting the Lies of the Enemy: 12 Scriptural Truths to Declare Over Your Disappointments. [online] Available at: https://go.lysaterkeurst.com/fight-the-lies-of-the-enemy/ [Accessed 19 Jan. 2019].

[27] MAD tv (n.d.). MAD tv - Bon Qui Qui at King Burger. [video] Available at: https://www.youtube.com/watch?v=jZkdcYlOn5M [Accessed 19 Jan. 2019].

[28] Goodreads.com. (n.d.). A quote from Charlotte Brontë, "Jayne Eyre". [online] Available at: https://www.goodreads.com/quotes/8596409-every-grievance-you-hold-hides-a-little-more-of-the [Accessed 19 Jan. 2019].

[29] Goodreads.com. (n.d.). A quote from Fyodor Dostoyevsky, "The Brothers Karamazov". [online] Available at: https://www.goodreads.com/quotes/366543-the-mystery-of-human-existence-lies-not-in-just-staying [Accessed 19 Jan. 2019].

[30] Beliefnet.com. (n.d.). The Lord's Prayer. [online] Available at: https://www.beliefnet.com/prayers/catholic/childrens-prayers/the-lords-prayer.aspx [Accessed 19 Jan. 2019].

CPSIA information can be obtained
at www.ICGtesting.com
Printed in the USA
BVHW081520180319
542952BV00009B/1325/P